# BIBLE CRAWLING

# BIBLE CRAWLING

Finding Joy in God by Journaling through the Psalms

## OLAN STUBBS

Foreword by David Mathis

RESOURCE *Publications* · Eugene, Oregon

Resource Publications
An Imprint of Wipf and Stock Publishers
199 W. 8th Ave., Suite 3
Eugene, OR 97401

www.wipfandstock.com

PAPERBACK ISBN: 978-1-6667-6147-4
HARDCOVER ISBN: 978-1-6667-6148-1
EBOOK ISBN: 978-1-6667-6149-8

01/06/23

This book is dedicated to my mom and dad who taught me, but more importantly modeled for me, how to read, study, memorize, meditate on, and journal through the Psalms.

"It's important to remember that in prayer the most important thing isn't to express ourselves, but to answer God and psalms help us do that, we answer the concerns on his heart while we express ours."

—EUGENE PETERSON

Meditation is "a form of mental prayer that involves some thinking about the meaning of the text and some personal response."

—FATHER JOSEPH KOTERSKI, associate professor of philosophy at Fordham University

The most important thing I had to do was to give myself to the reading of the Word of God and to meditation on it, that thus my heart might be comforted, encouraged, warned, reproved, instructed; and that thus, whilst meditating, my heart might be brought into experimental, communion with the Lord. I began, therefore, to meditate on the New Testament, from the beginning, early in the morning . . . searching, as it were, into every verse, to get blessing out of it . . . for the sake of obtaining food for my own soul. The result I have found to be almost invariably this, that after a very few minutes my soul has been led to confession, or to thanksgiving, or to intercession, or to supplication; so that though I did not, as it were, give myself to prayer, but to meditation, yet it turned almost immediately more or less into prayer.

When thus I have been for a while making confession, or intercession, or supplication, or have given thanks, I go on to the next words or verse, turning all, as I go on, into prayer for myself or others, as the Word may lead to it; but still continually keeping before me, that food for my own soul is the object of my meditation. The result of this is, that there is always a good deal of confession, thanksgiving, supplication or intercession mingled with my meditation, and that my inner man almost invariably is even sensibly nourished and strengthened and that by breakfast time, with rare exceptions, I am in peaceful if not happy state of heart . . . The difference between my former practice and my present one is this. Formerly, when I rose, I began to pray as soon as possible, and generally spent all my time till breakfast in prayer, or almost all the time. At all events I almost invariably began with prayer . . . But what was the result? I often spent a quarter of an hour, or half an hour, or even an hour on my knees, before being conscious to myself of having derived comfort, encouragement, humbling of soul, etc.; and often after having suffered from wandering of mind for the first ten minutes, or a quarter of an hour, or even half an hour, I only then began to pray.

I scarcely ever suffer in this way. For my heart being nourished by the truth, being brought into experimental fellowship with God, I speak to my Father, and to my Friend . . . about the things that He has brought before me in His precious Word . . . it is as plain to me as anything, that the first thing the child of God has to do morning by morning is to obtain food for his inner man . . . [Which is] not prayer, but the Word of God; and here again not the simple reading of the Word of God, so that It only passes through our minds, just as water runs through a pipe, but considering what we read, pondering over it, and applying it to our hearts."[1]

How can we turn our knowledge *about* God into knowledge *of* God? The rule for doing this is demanding, but simple. It is that we turn each truth that we learn *about* God into matter for meditation *before* God, leading to prayer and praise *to* God . . . Meditation is the activity of calling to mind, and thinking over, and dwelling on, and applying to oneself, the various things that one knows about the works and ways and purposes and promises of God. It is an activity of holy thought, consciously performed in the presence of God, under the eye of God, by the help of God, as a means of communion with God. Its purpose is to clear one's mental and spiritual vision of God, and to let His truth make its full and proper impact on one's mind and heart. It is a matter of talking to oneself about God and oneself; it is indeed often a matter of arguing with oneself, reasoning oneself out of moods of doubt and unbelief into a clear apprehension of God's power and grace."[2]

1. Muller, *Autobiography of George Mueller*, 15–24.
2. Packer, *Knowing God*, 18–19.

# Contents

CONTENTS

# Foreword

## By David Mathis

Are you ready to learn to crawl?

Crawling is a great concept for Bible intake. Far too many of us are moving far too quickly when we open God's word. Pressured in subtle and overt ways by modern life, and its implicit pace, many of us try to speed-walk; others just keep running. Most of us need to learn to crawl.

What I love about Olan's emphasis in this book is that *crawling* is slow and deliberate. Sure, you might "crawl," in a hurry, to safety, if you found yourself in a burning building. But typically when we say "crawl," we mean slow — moving but not very fast. When traffic is "crawling," well, it's not speeding along at the pace of modern life.

Bible readers today are typically operating at a pace that is far too swift. Olan has his finger on this need. According to *New York Times* columnist Thomas Friedman, we are living in "the age of accelerations." Our world has become increasingly fast-paced through the exponential development of technology and accompanying factors. Now "the pace of technology and scientific change," he writes, "outstrips the speed with which human beings and societies can usually adapt".[1] Friedman claims that "we are living through one of the greatest inflection points in history"[2] — perhaps unequaled in the last 500 years.

---

1. Friedman, *Thank You*, 39.
2. Friedman, *Thank You*, 3.

Maybe you've felt the effects, as I have. To-do lists seem to grow longer than we have time for. We hurry in the morning. Hurry on the road. Hurry at work. Hurry between meetings, and in meetings, and over meals. Hurry to get dinner ready. Hurry to eat. Hurry to get the kids cleaned up, and out the door, and get back home, and get to bed. Then, hurry to do more on evenings and weekends than we realistically have time for. Then hurry to bed ourselves. Get too little sleep. And start it all over the next day.

Worst of all may be hurrying through Bible reading. God's word goes in one ear and out the other in less than one second flat, and we hurry into the day, with empty minds and hungry hearts. Sadly, hurried Bible reading does us very little good. In fact, it might even do us ill, by cultivating hard-to-break patterns and teaching us to neglect the heart. Even more important than what constant hurry is doing to our work lives, family lives, relationships, and emotional health, is what it's doing to our souls. The late Dallas Willard (1935–2013) sounded the alarm toward the end of his life: "Hurry is the great enemy of spiritual life in our day."

When we come to the Bible, as Olan seeks to help us in this book, we want to welcome God's Truth, his concepts, his mind and will and heart, to direct and shape our lives. We want to make an effort to *see the world through God's words*, rather than *God through the world's*. Apart from receiving his words in sufficient quantity, and with due priority, we will inevitably follow "the course of this world" (Ephesians 2:2) and "be conformed to this world" (Romans 12:2). In time, the world's patterns and voice and pace will rule us.

Coming to God, in Scripture, is critical, but so is *the pace at which we move* once we've come. Rushing in and out of our readings, at the speed of our world, will do our souls far less good than learning to let the cadence of God's words set our pace. But how might we do that? How might we let God himself set the pace? Consider (1) the design of ancient books, and especially the Bible, (2) how we are to read them, and (3) what effect our reading can have on us.

## DESIGN OF ANCIENT TEXTS

Unlike so many of our books today, and internet content, ancient texts were not written quickly, nor written to be read quickly. They were designed to be read slowly, enjoyed, reread, and meditated on. After all, they had to be copied by hand. So published words were precious. They were not meant to be read once, but over and over again. And the Christian Scriptures, of all texts, ancient and modern, reward rereading, and slow reading — which is what Olan encourages in this book.

Moreover, these are God's own words in the Bible. Written through his inspired prophets and apostles, the biblical text is fundamentally different than any other mere human text and deserves from us a distinct approach — which means, at least, *reading without rushing*. The Bible is God's breathed-out Book (2 Timothy 3:16), to be breathed in by us as we catch our breath for the day.

When we "slow down" and meditate, memorize, and study Scripture *at an unhurried, even leisurely pace*, we are not engaging with it in a foreign, unexpected way. God means for his word to be read slowly, meditated on, not speed-read.

## CALL TO COMPREHEND AND EXPERIENCE

Also, we will need to slow down, from our normal pace of reading the news and contemporary texts, so we might *comprehend* what the ancient writer, speaking for God, has to say. The Scriptures were written centuries, even millennia, before us — in places and times different than our own. And not only that, but the Bible is divine in its content. No biblical prophecy, Peter writes, "was ever produced by the will of man, but *men spoke from God* as they were carried along by the Holy Spirit" (2 Peter 1:21).

Not only is the Bible itself designed to be engaged differently — more slowly and repeatedly — than our published words today, but also we, as humans and moderns, need a *more careful, deliberate pace* to be able to *understand* what the words mean — and to *experience* the truth. Bible reading, and particularly meditation, is to be emotionally responsive.

For this reason, speed-reading and Bible-reading are a mismatch. When we have questions (as we often do) about the meaning of a word or phrase or sentence in context, we don't just keep going to finish the reading, check the box, and move on. Rather, we need margin to pause and ponder. We need to give ourselves time and space to ask the questions that keep us from understanding, and then seek answers.

## BE FED, NOT JUST INFORMED[3]

Finally, another aspect of not just *comprehending* the text of Scripture, but also *experiencing* it, might be captured under the banner of *Seek to be fed, not just informed*.

In the book *Meditation and Communion with God*, Jack Davis waves the flag for "a more reflective and leisurely engagement with Scripture" in our day. According to Davis, the nature of modern life, and the "information overload" we have through television, smartphones, and endless new media "makes a slow, unhurried, and reflective reading of Scripture more vital than ever."[4]

*Leisurely* does not mean passive. Quality reading can be leisurely, and enjoyable, while at the same time being careful and active. In fact, the two belong together. An unhurried pace gives space for careful observation and rumination, while active reading demands a certain slowness.

Over time, as we come to know ourselves, we learn what kind of pace and approach is most conducive to feeding our souls, not just informing our minds — what pace helps us catch our emotional breath and find our spiritual balance for the day to come — how to "gather a day's portion" (Exodus 16:4) of spiritual food for our souls. The mind typically works faster than the heart. A faster pace might stimulate the mind, while a slower pace gives room to engage, and satisfy, the heart.

I love that this book calls out "finding joy" as the lead idea in the subtitle. Yes, that is what we're doing. Jesus said, "I am the bread

---

3. Davis, *Meditation and Communion*, 20.
4. David, *Meditation and Communion*, 22.

of life; whoever comes to me shall not hunger, and whoever believes in me shall never thirst" (John 6:35). We come to God's word to be fed, to find joy, to fill and satisfy our souls.

## PUSH BACK AGAINST THE TIDE

Ask yourself, *How hurried are my devotions?* Do you prioritize a daily season for unhurried Bible meditation and prayer? And have you learned to crawl, moving at the pace of the text, or do you feel the pressure to do your devotions at the pace of modern life?

In our world of speed and acceleration, what good will it do the Christian soul, and our love for others, as we learn to push back against the tides of this world, and its patterns of hurry, with a life-giving daybreak routine of catching our breath by breathing in the breath of God, and breathing out to him in prayer?

This may be one of the most countercultural things you can do: go to bed without a screen, get up early, grab an old-school paper Bible, put your phone aside, and let the voice of God in the Scriptures fill your mind and heart at his pace, not the world's.

Let Olan, and the Psalms, teach you how to crawl.

# Preface

## Personal Prayer and Worship Life

Jesus taught us to pray, "Give us this day our daily bread." Christ expected us to have daily time alone with him in prayer (Matthew 6:6–11). Most Christians seem to struggle with the consistency of this practice and the depth of their experience of God in prayer.

I really started walking with the Lord in high school. I heard Christians should have a personal prayer time to meet with God, yet I was very inconsistent. I tried different devotional books with measures of success but they never seemed to work for long. A greater problem was that I did not feel I was really meeting with God and worshipping him. It mostly seemed like I merely added new information to my mind about God. My mind grew but my heart was rarely stirred or warmed. There was not enough direct interaction with the Lord through his word.

My parents were very consistent in their time alone with the Lord. Dad would often read five psalms and a Proverb a day. Both wrote out their prayers and seemed to really grow in loving God with their mind, as well as their heart and soul. I asked dad how this had become a reality in his life.

He told me he heard Charles Stanley (the long time senior pastor of 1st Baptist Church in downtown Atlanta, Georgia) say, "If you'll give God thirty minutes a day in prayer every day he will radically change your life." Dad said, "I started that ten years ago. God really has changed my whole life." I was probably sixteen years old, zealous, and overconfident so naturally I said, "I'm going to do that!"

The first few months I probably attempted this every other day. It was closer to twenty minutes. I often slept half the time and daydreamed the other half. But I do have distinct memories of coming home after school, going to my room, reading my Bible, and praying, "Jesus, when you walked on earth your disciples asked you 'Teach us to pray' and you did. Teach me."

After months of perseverance, my time in prayer became more consistent, though not daily. Sometimes thirty minutes would fly by and I naturally wanted to spend more time alone with the Lord. This practice has continued in my life for many years now by God's grace.

## PLAN

Someone said, "If you aim at nothing you'll hit it every time." Having a realistic plan for personal time alone with the Lord can be a game changer. Otherwise you are likely to flounder.

## WHAT TO PRAY

I try to consistently read through the Bible taking one or two chapters a day just to read. It's best for me to have a smaller portion to go deeper. Short Bible reading and study leads to meditation, which leads to prayer, which leads to worship, which leads to life change.

I primarily focus on a psalm or a portion of a psalm every day no matter what else in the Bible I may be reading at that time. Sometimes I only use six to twelve verses if the psalm is longer. I'll usually read a very short portion of a commentary or devotional on that psalm so that I have a good understanding of what is going on. Context in God's word is crucial to understand the passage.

Then I'll read the psalm verse by verse while journaling along with the psalm. If I'm reading Psalm 1:1 I'll take the truth of that verse and turn it into a personal prayer for myself. I might write down "Lord I want to be blessed by you. Give me wisdom about things and people I allow to influence me. If there's anything I'm watching on TV or listening to on the radio that is influencing me to sin please convict me."

The Psalms are prayers, meditations and worship songs. If you want to pray, meditate, and worship the Lord, Psalms may be the best way to naturally do that. Any portion of God's Word can be a diving board into prayer but the Psalms seem best, because most were originally written as prayers, meditations, and worship songs. Because of this it is more natural to turn them into fuel for our own prayers, meditations, and worship songs. Tim Keller, the Manhattan based pastor and author, says "All theologians and leaders of the church have believed that the Psalms should be used and reused in every Christian's daily private approach to God . . . The Psalms are the divinely ordained way to learn devotion to God."[1] Matthew Henry, the great Bible commentator, says about the Psalms: "this book is of singular use to convey divine life and power, and a holy warmth, into our affections."[2]

Listen to Dane Ortlund's wise advice on the importance of daily Bible reading focused on the Psalms.

> *Make the Bible your central daily ritual.* Make it your habit without which you have not lived a normal day. By no means allow this to become a law towering over and condemning you . . . Fight to stay healthy. Stay hooked up to the IV of gospel and help and counsel and promise by reading the Bible each day . . . take your asthmatic soul in one hand and the oxygen tank of the Bible in your other hand, and bring the two together. Reading the Bible is inhaling . . . prayer is exhaling . . . the most effective way to pray is to turn your Bible reading into prayer . . . the Psalms are the one book in the Bible addressed to God. In it God takes us by the hand and gives us word to speak back to him . . . Never go too long without making them your own prayers.[3]

---

1. Keller, *Songs of Jesus*, vii.
2. Henry, *Henry Commentary*, 604.
3. Ortlund, *Deeper*, 15–25.

## WHEN TO PRAY

For many the morning is the best time to meet with God, with more silence and potential to influence your whole day. But the Bible never says mornings are always better for private prayer. Choose the time that works best for you.

I try to meet with God personally first thing in the day. Sometimes a busy schedule or a tired body prevents this. Then I'll try and take the first free time I have later in the day, whether that is a lunch break or ten pm after all kids are in bed, to pull away and meet with God.

## HOW TO PRAY

If you struggle with consistency, there is probably some lack of delight in your prayer life. That is common and yet sinful. We must repent and ask for the grace of Christ to forgive us and change us.

Make a plan and commit to it. Ask for accountability. Maybe even start by praying with others more disciplined and delighted in this area. Persevere in prayer even when you don't feel like it. Beg God to change your desires.

I often start to pray with minimal desire and more discipline. By God's grace as I persevere in faithfulness God draws near. James 4:8 is a promise I claim in prayer often. Do all you can to meet with the Lord in his word and prayer and see if he does not draw near to you and change you.

Desire plus discipline will eventually lead to delight (Psalm 37:4). One of the main things that we should pray for is to be conformed to the image of Christ. Jesus loved to be alone with his Father (Luke 5:16). So should we. Beg the Lord to change your heart until you love to pray, long to meditate, and anticipate times of private worship. If Christ on earth needed a regular pattern of prayer, certainly we do.

God loves to give good gifts to his children. Discipline and delight in prayer are two gifts to ask for. "You will seek me and you will find me, when you seek me with all your heart." Jeremiah 29:13.

I've written this book as a primer of sorts on prayer, meditation, and personal worship. The goal would be to go through it in a month to train yourself in a regular time of praying through journaling, meditating on, and worshipping through the Psalms. Hopefully this can help set a life-long pattern for your life.

# Acknowledgments

I would like to thank everyone at Wipf and Stock for working with me to publish this book. I would like to thank Sylvia Welch for editing it for me so well. I would also like to thank Bob Smart and Harrison Perkins on encouraging me to write and publish, as well as giving me feedback and help along the way.

Shane Terrell mentored me in college. He led a missions trip to Brazil I participated in. He would regularly have all of us sit in a circle and open our Bibles to a psalm. We would each read a verse out loud and then put it into our own words in the form of a prayer. This practice had a profound influence in shaping my prayer life.

I also want to thank Lynna, my wife and best friend, as well as my four children for supporting me and allowing me the time to work on this project. I am really indebted to my mother and father as I said in the dedication. Their example more than anything, humanly speaking, has laid the foundation in my life for such a prayer life. Lastly, and most of all, I want to thank the Lord Jesus Christ for saving me, sanctifying me (slowly but surely), and enabling me to walk with him and write such a work. I hope and pray it blesses others as he has so richly blessed me.

# Introduction

## C.R.A.W.L.ing through the Bible

The college ministry I work for focuses on evangelism and discipleship. Most of the students in our ministry either came to Christ through the ministry or were very young in their faith when they first got involved. One of the first things we always emphasize with a new Christian is the importance of personal Bible reading. Every Christian should ideally meditate on God's word daily (Joshua 1:8, Psalm 1:1-2). Methods for this abound. Matthew Henry teaches, "To meditate in God's word is to discourse with ourselves concerning the great things contained in it, with a close application of mind, a fixedness of thought, till we be suitably affected with those things and experience the savour and power of them in our hearts."[1]

There are several problems that seem most common in Bible meditation and prayer for new believers and many more mature believers as well. One, they don't feel they have the time. Second, they don't know exactly where to start or what to do. Third, there seems to be tension between going super deep in one passage versus also reading broadly to cover lots of territory. I have developed an acronym (C.R.A.W.L.) that helps bring depth in Bible reading, while emphasizing humility and slowing down. The reality is that I believe this approach can help any Christian of any maturity level.

---

1. Henry, *Henry Commentary*, 605.

## HUMBLY

Babies crawl before they walk. There's no one right way to read the Bible but some ways are more helpful than others. This method is not meant to box anyone in. Rather it is like learning to play "chop sticks" on the piano before you attempt Beethoven. It's important to approach the Bible with a humble and teachable attitude. It's also helpful to make sure to set aside adequate time for this daily discipline as mentioned in the preface.

I also like the idea of crawling because it can imply going deep and plumbing the depths of Scripture. Imagine a miner digging deep in the earth to find rare jewels. At some point the cave might become so low and tight that he is forced to crawl on his knees or even his stomach to go deeper into the mine. We should be willing to humble ourselves to do the hard work of digging deeply in God's words to find the spiritual jewels there. John Piper, the Baptist pastor and author, says "Raking is easier than digging, but you only get leaves. If you dig you may get diamonds."[2] We must be willing to do the hard and humbling work of digging in the Word to find the diamonds of truth God has for us daily. Go low and go slow.

## SLOWLY

I often tell students there will never seem to be enough time to pray, worship, and meditate on the Bible. They will have to intentionally make time. They must make reading God's word a high priority in their lives. Setting aside 30 minutes a day for Bible meditation and prayer is a great goal. There's nothing magical or legalistic about this number. But most people will easily spend 30 minutes watching TV, working out, or getting ready in the morning. Surely time alone with God in His word is more valuable.

Once time is set aside though we must still learn to slow down. Modern society is so fast-paced that a huge danger in Bible reading is to speed through it too fast. A "Read through the Bible in a year" plan can be great. It can also be dangerous if it leads you to breeze through God's word at record pace without stopping to smell the

2. Piper, *When I Don't Desire God*, 12.

flowers of His truth and glory. There's a danger of doing whatever it takes to read your four chapters a day to check the box and thus miss God in the process.

## Chapter and Context

For the Bible reading plan I'm suggesting it's ideal to choose one chapter a day to read. Sometimes only a few verses will do. Other times two chapters may fit. But in general, choose a chapter a day to go deep with. Better to go a mile deep and an inch wide than the other way around when it comes to Bible meditation.

It's best to know the context of what you're reading before you dive in. You don't need a seminary education to understand and apply God's word. But there is a difference in how one should approach a paradox in Proverbs and an argument from one of Job's friends. Reading Jesus's parables is different than trying to understand Revelation.

It's not ideal for your daily Bible reading to become so focused on in-depth academic study that you don't have time to warm your heart with the heat of God's goodness radiating in Scripture. But it is helpful to have a general idea of the text before you approach it. Commentaries such as Matthew Henry's or Derek Kidner's are short enough and insightful enough to be helpful on various passages of Scripture. A good study Bible can be a great help here as well.

I try to start my day with a psalm. The Psalms, more than any other book of the Bible, are designed to be prayed personally. Not only this, but they are perfectly designed to directly impact our emotions and desires. Keller says "we are to be immersed in them so that they profoundly shape how we relate to God . . . They are written to be prayed, recited, and sung- to be *done*, not merely to be read."[3]

If I was reading Psalm 1 for the first time, reading a short commentary or devotional on the passage would probably point me to the fact that the word "Blessed" literally means "happy." This is a very helpful insight. Many would be very tempted to breeze past the word "Blessed" as some spiritual sounding word that had

---

3. Keller, *Songs of Jesus*, vii-viii.

little meaning to them. They might think of their grandma saying "Bless you!" when they sneezed. This probably wouldn't stir many spiritual affections.

But if they realize the word means to be truly and holistically happy they might literally begin to feel their heart perk up with desire as they think "Happy?! I want to be happy! My whole life is about being happy! I didn't know the Bible would speak so directly to that!" Before they've even begun to read their appetite has already become enticed by briefly understanding the ancient context and words.

## Read and Remember

After a brief bit of context, dive into the word for yourself. Truly nothing is better than this. Reading the very words of God in your own language is a privilege that throughout the ages, many believers haven't had. Sometimes one verse or phrase is more than enough to consume your heart and mind. Remember to read slowly. The goal is not just gaining information but rather supernatural transformation (2 Corinthians 3:18). Keller teaches that meditation "is taking words of the Scripture and pondering them in such a way that your thoughts and feelings converge on God."[4] Too many people may read four chapters of the Bible a day but remember little of what they read. Or, they may remember much but apply little.

Supposedly A. W. Tozer, a great Bible teacher of the last century, would read (whether the Bible or other books) until he sensed the Holy Spirit impressing something on his soul. Then he would stop and pray and meditate and worship.[5] That is an incredible approach that will benefit us deeply if we can apply it.

Psalm 1 is a short psalm, but I could easily spend thirty minutes just focused on the first two verses. I would probably slow down and read those two verses three or four times. I am trying to soak up all the meaning I can find. I prayerfully want to drain the

4. Keller, *Prayer,* 90.
5. Snyder, *In Pursuit of God,* 83.

words of their meaning and implications for my life. I would probably be drawn to verse two specifically.

"But his delight is in the law of the Lord and on his law he meditates day and night." If I attempt to drill down into the depth of the verse with my mind as I read, I'm not just reading about meditation, I'm actually meditating. Here was a life changing thought I had one day while meditating on that verse. "Meditating day and night is all consuming. It seems impossible. Unless I have super strong emotions towards something that keeps my mind laser focused on that topic I don't think I can do it. But if I miss my wife while I'm away on a trip, I'll find my mind naturally drawn to her and thinking of her. I won't even have to try to meditate on her. It will naturally happen. That must be a key to meditating on God's word! Of course there's a place for discipline and focus. But if I fall passionately in love with God and his word my mind will often naturally be drawn to meditate on it without even having to try!" Simply taking the time to read the Bible slowly and think about all the clauses and connections can truly change your life.

## Ask and Answer

As you read, ask questions of the text. Interact with the text. Don't breeze past challenging sentences. Slow down. Pause. Wonder. Ask what it meant to the original audience. Why did the human author choose that word? Why did the Holy Spirit ordain that phrase to be repeated? As plausible answers come to your mind write them down.

Pray and ask the Holy Spirit to draw near to you as you draw near to him via the word (James 4:8). Ask him to convict you and enlighten you. Pray Psalm 119:18 "Open my eyes, that I may behold wondrous things out of your law."

From Psalm 1:1 I would ask "How am I being influenced by sinful men? Please convict me Holy Spirit of any and all ways that I'm sinfully influenced by sinful men etc. . . . " As I read Psalm 1:2 I might ask, "Is there any specific discipline I need to employ to find my joy more in the Bible and less in TV?" As ideas come to mind I would jot them down.

If I made it to Psalm 1:3 I might ask questions like these: "How is my life supposed to be like a tree planted by streams of water? What does it mean that I'll prosper in all I do? This isn't teaching prosperity gospel theology is it? Lord, give me wisdom to understand your word as you promise in James 1:5! I can't do it alone!"

## Write and Worship

The best way for me to slow down and interact with the text is to write. Jumbled thoughts often become clear and untangled through the end of a pen. I may have already begun writing as I am asking the above questions, but now I'll move even further into true meditation. I take each verse and prayerfully meditate on the meaning. I begin to write it in my own words, turning it into a personal prayer.

If I was reading Psalm 1:1 I might write, "Lord, I want you to bless me. I need your blessings! I am so weak! Left to myself I will be overcome by the influence of sinful men."

If you read something beautiful, stop and savor it. If you read something convicting, stop and repent. JI Packer said, "How can we turn our knowledge about God into knowledge of God? The rule for doing this is simple but demanding. It is that we turn each Truth that we learn about God into matter for meditation before God, leading to prayer and praise to God."[6]

Somewhere in the writing is where I usually begin to sense that I am meditating. David Mathis, who writes for Desiring God ministries, says we should chew on biblical truth "until we begin to feel some of its magnitude in our hearts."[7] He also says that we should seek to "emotionally glory in what [we] understand," and "press it deeply into our feelings."[8] This type of meditation is a great measuring stick of our daily time alone with the Lord. Ideally, it should bring us to the real goal that should be the daily pinnacle of our daily meditation: worship.

---

6. Packer, *Knowing God*, 18 19.

7. Mathis, *Habits of Grace*, 56.

8. Mathis, *Habits of Grace*, 45, 55.

John Calvin, one of the greatest theologians of all time, is helpful on this point as well. He states "believers know by use and experience that ardor burns low unless they supply new fuel. Accordingly, among our prayers, meditation both on God's nature and on his Word is by no means superfluous. And so by David's example, let us not disdain to insert something that may refresh our languishing spirits with new vigor."[9] Trying to sit still and focus and pray for thirty minutes straight can be hard and overwhelming, if not impossible for some of us. But when our prayers are mixed with meditations on God and his word, as the Psalms often are, our prayers can become hot, as if new logs were continually being thrown on the fire.

Worship is about awe, wonder, love and praise. Tozer says "Worship . . . is to feel in your heart and express in some appropriate manner a humbling but delightful sense of admiring awe and astonished wonder and overpowering love in presence of . . . Our Father in Heaven."[10] Hopefully as I read, write, ask, and answer it will be like turning a diamond to see the different facets of beauty as the light hits it from different angles. God's word is eternally deep. You will never exhaust it in this lifetime. There is enough glory there to ponder for all time. As you learn more about the Lord it should raise the affections of your heart in joyous worship and thanksgiving. As we worship we should be conformed into His image as 2 Corinthians 3:18 teaches. Truly beholding Christ leads to slowly but surely becoming like Christ.

John Owen was another one of the greatest theologians of all times. He says that "meditation is the affecting of our own hearts and minds with love, delight, and [humility] . . . It is better that our affections exceed our light from the corruption of our understandings, than that our light exceed our affections from the corruption of our wills." Why is this so? Because if our affections are not involved real spiritual growth and sanctification will not happen.[11]

9. Calvin, *Institutes*, 867.

10. Snyder, *In Pursuit of God*, 149.

11. Quoted in Keller, *Prayer*, 152, 182, 247.

## Listen and Learn

As we read slowly, we should be learning. We should be gleaning new knowledge. This is not mere academic knowledge, but true knowledge of God that may start with academic study. However, it won't stop there. Truth should enter our minds as a doorway to our hearts to stir our affections and capture our will for God's glory. We should be "seeking to have that truth shape and permeate our reality."[12]

I say listen as well because Martin Luther taught that sometimes in prayer and Bible study the Holy Spirit will "preach in your heart with rich, enlightening thoughts."[13] This does not mean that the Holy Spirit will give any new revelation. Tim Keller comments, "Luther is talking about the eyes of our hearts being enlightened (Ephesians 1:18) so that things we know with the mind become more fully rooted in our being's core."[14] Calvin says it this way. "[W]e do not with perverted ardor and without discrimination rashly seize upon what first springs to our minds. Rather, after diligently meditating upon it, we embrace the meaning which the Spirit of God offers."[15] Martyn Lloyd-Jones, the great London pastor of the last century, simply states "listen to the voice of God as He speaks through the Spirit that is within you."[16]

The personal insight I shared under the *Read and Remember* heading above didn't come from a special day where I planned to fast and pray and try extra hard at meditation. It came from a fairly normal day of prayer and Bible study where it seemed that the Holy Spirit showed up in a more unique way and engaged my mind. The insights seemed to come so naturally that day, it was like the Holy Spirit was "preaching" to my mind. Consistency and quantity of time alone with the Lord will often, eventually lead to quality of time with the Lord. Don't ever try to play quality time against quantity of time with God. Both are needed.

12. Mathis, *Habits of Grace*, 42.

13. Parrish, *A Simple Way to Pray*, 25, 35, 50.

14. Keller, *Prayer*, 96.

15. Calvin, *Institutes*, lvi.

16. Lloyd-Jones, *Spiritual Depressions*, 114.

This won't happen every day, but we should be sensitive to when it does. All the more reason to take our time C.R.A.W.L.ing through the Bible in hopes of meeting God in a fresh way. Pray earnestly that he will draw near daily!

## CONCLUSION

I might end my study of Psalm 1 for the day by realizing that my love for God's word flows from my love for Christ. I love the Bible because it tells me of my Savior. The Bible continually convicts me of sin and reminds me of his amazing grace, thus drawing me closer to him.

Ultimately, the goal of all this is to see the glory of Christ in a fresh way daily. To love and worship him more and thus to be slowly but surely more conformed to his image in all we do, think, say, and feel (2 Corinthians 3:18). If you don't have a good consistent habit of Bible reading and meditation or if your current plan has gotten stale, I encourage you to try C.R.A.W.L.ing for a month. This book is intended to help you do that.

Each short chapter will give you enough context to hopefully not be confused by the psalm for the day. Then there should be space for you to "journal through the psalm," essentially writing a prayer based on it, in your own words and considering the circumstances of your daily life. (If there's not enough room for you, use a journal with this study.) Lastly we will conclude each day with an old hymn. The idea is to end by singing (whether out loud or in our hearts) in true worship to the Lord. If you don't know the hymn or the "tune" that goes with it, simply read and meditate on the words.

Sometimes the Lord may "speak" to us in a unique or fresh way as we noted above. Many days we probably will not experience that and this is ok. But it should be the goal and desire of our heart each day to truly worship the Lord through his word.

# Day 1 Psalm 1

## CHAPTER AND CONTEXT

This psalm was intentionally put at the beginning of the entire book of Psalms as an introduction. Tim Keller says that it is "a meditation on meditation."[1] It opens the Psalter to us in a way that says, if you will take time to meditate on this whole book you will be richly blessed.

This psalm starts by focusing on the fact that all human beings are influenced by others. None of us are truly an island. Who and what we are influenced by can truly set the trajectory of our lives. We should not passively allow others to influence. We must proactively guard our hearts by guarding our eyes and ears.

Further we must intentionally make sure that the main thing influencing us is the word of God, not the nightly news, not the latest cultural fad, nor the hottest bestselling book off the shelf. We must aggressively, daily pursue God through his word. This will be time intensive and often hard but always worth it.

If we daily meditate on God's word we will bear fruit for his glory and our joy. It will change our lives. Others will eventually be able to notice. We will bear fruit according to seasons. That does not mean that we will always be bearing one hundred fold fruit. There will be hard seasons, dry, dusty, hot, and hard. When a drought comes and a tree stays alive that is a success in and of itself.

This psalm promises that God's word will be for us like an internal and subterranean stream that will never dry up no matter what, if we are purposeful to meditate on it daily. We must plumb its depths. We must do the hard work to drill down to the core of the meaning of the words. But if we do, even "when all around our soul gives way," God's word will be our "hope and stay."[2]

---

1. Keller, *Praying with the Psalms*, 14.
2. Mote, "The Solid Rock," 402.

There will be many days, times and seasons where you do not feel like you are prospering but if you will persevere in the discipline of meditating, you will prosper spiritually whether you feel it or not. This psalm is not guaranteeing physical or material prosperity. It is promising that by God's word and grace we will flourish spiritually, which should matter most to us.

The righteous person meditates on God's word daily and thus prospers spiritually. The wicked have the opposite experience. Biblically speaking "wicked" people are not just the worst sinners such as murderers and rapists. No, biblically speaking we are all wicked and sinful and deserving God's wrath. Anyone who does not seek to truly trust in and follow the one true God is considered wicked even if their outward life seems moral and nice.

The wicked may prosper in many ways but not spiritually. They are compared to chaff. Chaff refers to the husks of a wheat crop. When the wheat was harvested it had to be separated from the chaff. The chaff eventually was blown away by the wind. It was useless. The wheat was saved and later consumed for nourishment.

The blessed person's life will flourish spiritually and be pleasing to the Lord. God will know and enjoy these people intimately. The wicked person will eventually perish eternally in hell for all eternity unless they repent.

The reality is only one truly righteous man has ever lived. His name was Jesus. But at the end of his life he was blown away by the wrath of God on the cross, not for his own sins, but for the sins of his people. But he was also resurrected to stand again in the assembly of the righteous.

If we repent of our sins and trust in his life and death as our substitute we can be found righteous by grace in him. We can be raised to newness of life here and in the next life. Our lives will prosper spiritually for him now. We will stand with him in the assembly of the righteous if we are firmly planted in him.

## READ AND REMEMBER

With the above context in mind, read Psalm 1 once slowly.

## ASK AND ANSWER

Read Psalm 1 a second time, this time writing down any questions or insights you may have as you go.

## WRITE AND WORSHIP

Now, in light of these questions and insights, journal and pray through Psalm 1 below in your own words. Write out your worshipful meditation and prayer as you go. When you are done, spend a few moments singing the hymn that follows whether out loud or in your mind. All the while trust the Holy Spirit to speak to you and give you fresh insight as you go.

## COME, YE SINNERS, POOR AND NEEDY

by Joseph Hart

Come, ye sinners, poor and needy, Weak and wounded, sick and sore; Jesus ready stands to save you, Full of pity, love and pow'r.
Come, ye thirsty, come, and welcome, God's free bounty glorify; True belief and true repentance, Every grace that brings you nigh.
Let not conscience make you linger, Nor of fitness fondly dream; All the fitness He requireth Is to feel your need of Him.
Come, ye weary, heavy laden, Lost and ruined by the fall; If you tarry till you're better, You will never come at all.
I will arise and go to Jesus, He will embrace me in His arms; In the arms of my dear Savior, O, there are ten thousand charms.

## LISTEN AND LEARN

Write any final insights you have here.

# Day 2 Psalm 2

## CHAPTER AND CONTEXT

Psalm 2 was written about a godly king of Israel. He had multiple enemies attacking him. Second Samuel 10 describes such a scenario. The king may have felt outmatched and outnumbered. In that place, he turns to the Lord in prayer and meditation.

Our times of prayer and meditation should never just be going through the motions to check the box saying we read our Bibles for the day. Rather, we should look at time in the word and prayer as preparation for the spiritual battle we face each day. See Ephesians 6:10–20 and 1 Peter 5:7–9. We meditate on God's word to strengthen our soul for the battle we are in. It's similar to a soldier loading his gun for war.

A large part of our times with the Lord should be us being honest about our thoughts and feelings with him. We should bring all of our doubts, fears, and questions and pour them at his feet. We see the psalmist doing that in Psalm 2.

The psalmist looks out at his surrounding enemies and he has plenty of reasons to fear. At the human level there is plenty of evidence to say that he will be wiped out by these foreign nations. They hate God and therefore they hate the godly king ruling God's people.

In light of this specific situation the psalmist turns his eyes from earth to heaven. He doesn't have a vision of God on his throne. Rather he meditates on the fact that there is ultimately only one king who matters, the King of the universe. The one true living God sits on his throne and he is not bothered by all the nations threatening to attack God's people. In fact, God laughs at them. God is no more worried than a killer whale would be worried by a tadpole attacking him.

God's plans will always stand. He has ordained his king to rule on earth. He will not let him be overthrown. He will fight the ultimate battles for his peoples. He will pour out his wrath and anger on all his true enemies. The point is God is 100% confident of victory in the coming battle. As the psalmist meditates on God's confidence he becomes confident.

So much of good prayer and meditation is about getting our eyes off ourselves and onto God. We don't do this through pretending we don't have problems and stuffing our negative emotions. Rather, we pray honestly and humbly about all that bothers us but we don't stop there! Prayer shouldn't be just a venting session. Rather it should be a time to look past our venting to the God who is still on his throne.

God is a great God who will fight our battles for us and answer our prayers. He commands us to ask him for victories. God's ultimate plan is to take the whole world over for his glory. And he will be successful!

But here is the really great part. Not only is our God mighty, he is merciful. Any of his enemies who will repent and come to him can be forgiven. This is the ultimate reason to worship. The God of wrath, anger, and might is also a God of mercy and delight when we humbly acknowledge our sin and repent.

As exciting as this psalm is, there is a problem. There are many times in life where it does not seem like the Lord comes through for us. Many times he doesn't seem to fight our battles or answer our prayers. What are we to do then?

The clearest example of this is when the one true King of Israel, the Lord Jesus Christ came to earth and went to the cross. He cried out to the Father on the cross as the nations conspired against him. And His Father was silent and left him alone to suffer and die.

But we know why. God was working for our salvation behind the scenes. This is why an enemy of Christ can come and bow the knee and be protected from the well-deserved wrath of God. Because Christ took that wrath in the place of all who would trust in him.

When you feel as if the whole world is against you, turn the eyes of your heart to God in prayer. Remember the true King of Israel, seated on the throne. His enemies were conquered at the cross. Trust him to settle all accounts in his perfect timing and ways.

## READ AND REMEMBER

With the above context in mind, read Psalm 2 once slowly.

## ASK AND ANSWER

Read Psalm 2 a second time jotting down any thoughts, questions, or insights here or in the margins.

## WRITE AND WORSHIP

First read the example journal on Psalm 2 below. Then, in light of your own questions and insights, journal and pray through Psalm 2 below in your own words. Write out your worshipful meditation and prayer as you go. When you are done, spend a few moments singing the hymn that follows whether out loud or in your mind. All the while trust the Holy Spirit to speak to you and give you fresh insight as you go.

1. All people in this world apart from you are your enemies oh Lord. I was your enemy and should and could be still if you hadn't chosen to save, adopt, and sanctify me (Ephesians 1:3–5).
2. The most powerful men on earth often set themselves against you. This clearly happened Lord when you walked the earth.
3. All of us in our sin hate to be told what to do. We want to throw off your control and be our own master. Please convict me Lord of anywhere or way I'm doing this now. Don't let me live in subtle rebellion and not know it.
4. Even if all seven billion humans on earth today and all the angels in heaven rebel you'd have no worry or fear. You sit on your throne and laugh. You mock and scorn your hard hearted enemies. They can never touch your throne, your power, your plan (Daniel 4:35).

5. When you come in final judgement, men will flee in terror and beg mountains to fall on them and to hide them from the wrath of the Lamb (Revelation 6:16).

6. You ordained that David rule and then many of his descendants like Solomon, Asa, Jehosophat, and Hezekiah. But ultimately you've installed the one true godly King on your holy hill forever; the real King, the true Son of David, who'll reign forever. Jesus will eventually conquer all the earth and set the world at peace (Isaiah 2:4).

7. Jesus was eternally begotten but enthroned in a new way at the resurrection (Philippians 2:9-11).

8. Father you promised Jesus that he could ask you and you'd give him all the earth and that you'd give him people from every tongue, tribe, and nation (Revelation 7:9-11). I can come to you "in Christ" and join his prayer and have confidence. Give us souls from the nations! Use me to lead others to Christ!

9. You'll destroy your enemies through eternal hell or through breaking them and making them humble through saving grace.

10. All men should live in holy fear. Teach me to number my days and live humbly (Psalm 90:10-16).

11. Make me radically serious about obedience in all ways, including small ways like eating and drinking (1 Corinthians 10:31).

12. I worship you Savior who died and rose for me! I rest in your finished work.

## CROWN HIM WITH MANY CROWNS

by Matthew Bridges and Godfrey Thring

Crown Him with many crowns, The Lamb upon His throne: Hark! How the heav'nly anthem drowns All music but its own! Awake, my soul, and sing Of Him who died for thee, And hail Him as thy matchless King Thru all eternity.

Crown Him the Lord of love: Behold His hands and side- Rich wounds, yet visible above, In beauty glorified. No angel in the sky Can fully bear that sight, But downward bends his wondering eye At mysteries so bright.

Crown Him the Lord of life: Who triumphed o'er the grave, Who rose victorious to the strife For those He came to save. His glories now we sing, Who died and rose and high, Who died eternal life to bring And lives that death may die.

## LISTEN AND LEARN

Write any final insights you have here.

# Day 3 Psalm 3

## CHAPTER AND CONTEXT

With some psalms we know little of the context in which they were written. In others we know much. There is an important background story to understand to get the most out of Psalm 3.

Second Samuel 11 tells of King David's adultery with Bathsheba and his murdering her husband Uriah. In the next chapter God forgives David but says "I will raise up evil against you out of your own house" (2 Samuel 12:11). Second Samuel 15 tells the story of Absalom, David's son, seeking to violently overthrow his father. As David flees the city in 2 Samuel 16:7–10 one of his enemies curses him and David responds with great humility. It is an amazing story. You might should pause and read it right now.

As you come to Psalm 3 seek to put yourself in David's shoes. Many of us have experienced hardship. Few have experienced something so terrible as not only losing our job and home and city but also having our own son trying to murder and usurp us. The pain must have been nearly unbearable.

When you only read the historical books such as 2 Samuel, David often seems superhuman. We often see him handle hardship with amazing resilience and steadfastness. We see him respond to enemies with such grace and patience. How did he live so faithfully through so much suffering?

When you come to the psalms that David wrote during those years he often prays like a little child pouring out his heart, all of his woes, to his mom and dad. He seems broken, desperate, weak, and needy. Here is the secret to his strength. If we will be brutally honest with ourselves and with the Lord in the place of prayer, God will give us all the internal strength of soul we need to thrive even under the worst adversity.

Notice in Psalm 3:1–2 how he expresses his deepest emotions to the Lord. He feels overwhelmed and oppressed. Even worse, people are saying that God has left him. He must have felt abandoned by the Lord. People's taunts and words were searing his inner man. Often times we imagine that what others say about us reflects what God thinks about us. David probably wrestled with this. So he turned to God in heartfelt prayer.

He prays like a raw exposed nerve. God already knows all that is in our hearts. We might as well tell him. As we express our pain to the Lord something else often naturally happens. We get our eyes off of ourselves and our circumstances and onto the Lord. In him our confidence can start to rise.

In verse 3 the tone of the psalm changes from hurt to hope. God is his protector and the one who can and will restore him. God had made promises to David and David trusted in them. (See 2 Samuel 7 for some of those promises.)

In verse 4 David says he knows God answered his prayer. What exactly does that mean? How did God practically answer him? Look at the next two verses.

David was probably literally camped across a river from an army that wanted to kill him. He may have been able to hear their voices and see the smoke from their camp fires. Yet what does he do? He lays down and gets a great night of sleep. How in the world does he do that?

He has reminded himself through prayer and meditation that God has and will continue to fight his battles for him. He can rest. He is filled with internal peace, where once fear had reigned.

In verse 7 he asks God to fight for him. But he also reminds himself that the Lord has always done this for him in the past. He ends the psalm in hope that once again God will come through for him and for all his people. We can have the same confidence as we approach God in prayer through our Savior Christ.

## READ AND REMEMBER

With the above context in mind, read Psalm 3 once slowly.

## ASK AND ANSWER

Read Psalm 3 a second time jotting down any thoughts, questions or insights here or in the margins.

## WRITE AND WORSHIP

In light of your questions and insights, as well as the context above, journal and pray through Psalm 3 below in your own words. Make sure to honestly express all of your emotions to the Lord, the positive and the negative. Write out your worshipful meditation as you go. When you are done, spend a few moments singing the hymn that follows whether out loud or in your mind. All the while trust the Holy Spirit to speak to you and give you fresh insight as you go.

## THE SOLID ROCK

by Edward Mote

My hope is built on nothing less Than Jesus' blood and righteousness; I dare not trust the sweetest frame, But wholly lean on Jesus' name.

When darkness veils His lovely face, I rest on His unchanging grace; In ev'ry high and stormy gale My anchor holds within the veil.

His oath, His covenant, His blood Support me in the whelming flood; When all around my soul gives way, He then is all my hope and stay.

When He shall come with trumpet sound, O may I then in Him be found, Dressed in His righteousness alone, Faultless to stand before the throne.

On Christ, the solid Rock I stand- All other ground is sinking sand, All other ground is sinking sand.

## LISTEN AND LEARN

Write any final insights you have here.

# Day 4 Psalm 4

## CHAPTER AND CONTEXT

We do not know the exact context of this psalm but we do know it was written under duress. It may have been written during the same situation that produced Psalm 3. One of the most important lessons to learn in prayer and meditation is to strive to always be brutally honest with the Lord and ourselves.

We often like to paint a rosier picture of reality to ourselves and those around us. Many of us are not comfortable with negative emotions. We stuff and stifle them. But eventually they will bubble up and usually in unhealthy ways. A much more productive strategy is to slow down, get before Christ mentally, and pour out all our thoughts, feelings, and desires to him in an unfiltered manner. He can handle it. Not only that, he will meet us there and grow us as we do.

David begins this prayer begging God to hear him and move on his behalf. As he asks for present deliverance, he wisely reminds himself that God has often come through for him in the past. Preaching our own history to ourselves can be a powerful, almost tangible reminder of the goodness and faithfulness of God in our lives. This often serves to lift our spirits as they sink under our present hardships.

The reality is that our thoughts and feelings are not only impacted by ourselves and God. We are highly influenced by the words and deeds of others. David is honest about this in his prayers.

In verse 2 David is probably speaking to his enemies, not literally but in his head. Do we not all do this at times? We think about what we would like to say if we had the chance. Rather than merely talking to ourselves about how we might hypothetically tell them off if we had the chance, we should rather prayerfully think through what we want to say and why.

David's name is being drug through the mud. At least part of what is being said about him is falsehood. It hurts him as much as it would hurt any of us. He wants it to end. He's processing his emotions with the Lord, before the Lord. We must learn to do the same.

In verse 3 he returns to his meditation. God is real. God is good. God is for me. He is powerful. He will save. He will vindicate me in the right time and way. I don't have to ultimately fight the battle for my honor and name. God will fight for me.

Verse 4 is interesting because it may be addressed to David's enemies or it may be addressed to his own men who are angry and spoiling for a fight. Either way its ultimate impact on us is the same. There is a righteous time and manner to be angry. But even godly anger can quickly turn to sinful anger if we don't steward it well.

David is saying think before you act. Be wise. Slow down. Consider your anger. Why are you angry? Are you right to be angry? Is it best for you to take matters into your own hands now? Or is it better to wait on God's plans and timing? These are great questions for us to ask ourselves especially when we struggle with anger. (God even asked some of these in Jonah 4.)

Rather than letting rash emotions drive us to rash actions, prayer can calm us down. Meditation can remind us. Writing down our thoughts, feelings, and prayers can help to refocus us on truth. Worshipping and trusting God is the safe place we must strive to always remain internally.

In verse 6 David returns to his prayers. Many had spoken of David saying that there was no hope for him. People kept saying that he was finished. His life and his rule were over. Rather than trying to get into an argument and defend himself, he turns his heart and soul to his Savior. "Smile on me Lord! Make your presence clear and known to me." As he turns his face metaphorically to the Lord he begins to worship. He feels a sense of joy and delight. Gladness rises in his heart. This should be our goal in prayer daily! God's nearness is greater than any tangible gift we receive in this life. Listen to John Calvin: "This light, by a beautiful metaphor, is said to be *lifted up,* when, shining in our hearts, it produces trust and hope. It would not be enough for us to be beloved by God, unless the sense of this love came home to our hearts; but, shining upon them by the Holy Spirit, he cheers us with true and solid joy."[1]

This leads to true peace. Internal and external rest have been achieved by meeting with God. He ends with an affirmation. Only God can save. Only he can deliver. Only he can turn our panic to praise and our complaining into confidence.

## READ AND REMEMBER

With the above context in mind, read Psalm 4 once slowly.

## ASK AND ANSWER

Read Psalm 4 a second time jotting down any thoughts, questions, or insights here or in the margins.

## WRITE AND WORSHIP

In light of your questions and insights, as well as the context above, journal and pray through Psalm 4 below in your own words. Make sure to honestly express all of your emotions to the Lord, the good and the bad. Write out your worshipful meditation and prayer as you go. When you are done, spend a few moments singing the hymn that follows whether out loud or in your mind. All the while ask the Holy Spirit to speak to you and give you fresh insight as you go.

1. Calvin, *Psalms vol. 1*, 78–79.

# JESUS, I AM RESTING, RESTING

by Jean S. Pigott

Jesus, I am resting, resting In the joy of what Thou art; I am finding out the greatness Of Thy loving heart. Thou hast bid me gaze upon Thee, And Thy beauty fills my soul, For by Thy transforming power, Thou hast made me whole.

O, how great Thy loving kindness, Vaster, broader than the sea! O, how marvelous Thy goodness, Lavished all on me! Yes, I rest in Thee, Beloved, Know what wealth of grace is Thine, Know Thy certainty of promise, And have made it mine.

Simply trusting Thee, Lord Jesus, I behold Thee as Thou art, And Thy love, so pure, so changeless, Satisfies my heart; Satisfies its deepest longings, Meets, supplies its every need, Compasseth me round with blessings: Thin is love indeed!

Ever lift Thy face upon me As I work and wait for Thee; Resting 'neath Thy smile, Lord Jesus, Earth's dark shadows flee. Brightness of my Father's glory, Sunshine of my Father's face, Keep me ever trusting, resting, Fill me with Thy grace.

Jesus, I am resting, resting In the joy of what Thou art; I am finding out the greatness Of Thy loving heart.

## LISTEN AND LEARN

Write any final insights you have here.

# Day 5 Psalm 7

## CHAPTER AND CONTEXT

Cush (see the title of Psalm 7 in your Bible) was almost certainly either a supporter of King Saul or of Absalom. This psalm was written in a time of distress and persecution when someone was cursing David in similar ways to those we have discussed in the previous two days. The first two verses start in much the same way with David crying to God for help. This should be a normal part of our prayer life, especially in times of hardship.

In verses 3–5 David basically proclaims his innocence before the Lord. He's essentially saying, "If I did something to these men and deserve punishment then I'll happily receive it. But I know that I didn't." This is another important theme to remember in the Psalms. When a psalmist speaks of his innocence he never means that he is sinlessly perfect before the throne of God. Rather he means, at the human level, I'm not guilty of what my enemies accuse me of. Saul accused David of trying to usurp the throne but it wasn't true. David had opportunities to kill Saul and chose not to. See 1 Samuel 24 as an example.

In verse 6 and following, David begins to pray for God to arise and fight his battles for him. He's asking for protection and most of us are very comfortable with that. He also asks God to vindicate him. David wants it to be known that he is innocent of the false accusations. We can understand that desire as well. But then David begins to pray in a way that may bother most of us. But we must not skip over it. These types of prayers are scattered throughout the Psalms and this is not an isolated instance.

If David only prayed that wicked men's evil schemes would be ended we could easily agree. David goes further and prays that God would bring an end to evil men. The verses that follow describe God using violent weapons to bring death on David's enemies. This bothers us for many reasons but mainly because Christ taught us to pray for our enemies. What are we to do with prayers like these?

Should we skip them? No. The reality is the Bible is teaching us how to best process righteous anger. There are evil people in this world who will never repent. Our main prayer for all people should be that they repent and are converted. That is the most glorious way for God to bring an end to evil men, to convert them into godly men! But that does not always happen.

This can seem wrong and selfish at first glance. But further meditation will show the genius of such prayer. Before we comment on the right ways to pray against our enemies we must first mention the wrong ways. It would be wrong to pray in a self-centered way that takes perverse pleasure in the pain of my enemies. Second, it would be sinful to pray from a self-righteous attitude assuming, "I am all good, they are all evil, and I can look down on them with pride and condemnation." No, these prayers ultimately can only rightly flow from our hearts when our hearts are full of love, grace, and humility. But when they flow from such a heart they are actually best for all involved. How can that be so? In numerous ways.

First, praying that God would punish my enemies for their sins is best for me because it takes the vengeance out of my hands. The only way that I can persevere in loving my enemies and not retaliating is to believe that God will finally punish all sin as it deserves. This keeps me from sinfully taking matters into my own hands. This is crucial.

Second, these prayers are best for others who are innocent at the human level. If you work for a cruel boss who takes advantage of you, it is highly likely he does the same thing to others. If you pray that he is fired and he is, you have not only prayed to see your situation improved but also that of all of your fellow employees.

Third, these prayers are actually best for the person you are praying for. Often God uses hardship in our lives to drive us to a point of brokenness, desperation, and even salvation. See Psalm 83:16–18.

Lastly, these prayers are best for God's glory. When God returns and restores all things to perfection, all those who still persevere in sin will be finally eternally damned. This is actually part of what we pray when we pray, "Come quickly Lord Jesus" whether we know it or like it or not.

In conclusion, it is biblical to pray that God would judge our enemies. Vengeance isn't sinful. Vengeance just doesn't belong to us. It belongs to God (Romans 12:19, Hebrews 10:30). If you are still uncomfortable praying this way, at a minimum you can use these prayers to pray that God would finally bring an end to all of Satan's works, our true enemy. And then rest in confidence that Satan was defeated when Christ was judged by God's wrath in our place. Hallelujah, what a Savior! What a judge!

## READ AND REMEMBER

With the above context in mind, read Psalm 7 once slowly.

## ASK AND ANSWER

Read Psalm 7 a second time jotting down any thoughts, questions, or insights here or in the margins.

## WRITE AND WORSHIP

In light of your questions and insights, as well as the context above, journal and pray through Psalm 7 below in your own words. Specifically, think of anyone who seems to be your enemy in some sense. Make sure to honestly express all of your emotions to the Lord, the good and the bad. Write out your worshipful meditation and prayer as you go. If you do not have enough room, use a journal or the next page. When you are done, spend a few moments singing the hymn that follows whether out loud or in your mind. All the while ask the Holy Spirit to speak to you and give you fresh insight as you go.

# IT IS WELL WITH MY SOUL

by Horatio G. Spafford

When peace like a river attendeth my way, When sorrows like sea-billows roll; Whatever my lot, Thou hast taught me to say, "It is well, it is well with my soul."

Though Satan should buffet, tho' trials should come, Let this blest assurance control, That Christ has regarded my helpless estate, And hath shed His own blood for my soul.

My sin O, the bliss of this glorious thought, My sin not in part but that whole, Is nailed to the cross and I bear it no more, Praise the Lord, praise the Lord, O my soul!

And, Lord, haste the day when the faith shall be sight, The clouds be rolled back as a scroll, The trump shall resound and the Lord shall descend, "Even so"- it is well with my soul.

It is well It is well with my soul, with my soul, It is well, it is well with my soul.

## LISTEN AND LEARN

Write any final insights you have here.

# Day 6 Psalm 16

## CHAPTER AND CONTEXT

Most of the psalms we've looked at so far have primarily been prayers for help, for deliverance from hardships and enemies. This psalm is more of a meditation and rejoicing. It starts with a short prayer at the beginning but then moves to worship and praise.

In verse 2 David is meditating on the fact that all good gifts in this life come from the Lord. In verse 3 he specifically focuses on the blessings that God's people can be to us. A wonderful part of prayer is thanking God for specific blessings you have and continue to experience in life.

In verse 4 he pauses to look at the wicked. He does not seem to be in a place of fear or need. Rather he looks on them with pity. Whatever good things the wicked may experience in this life won't last. They seek other gods and in return get much sorrow. David pledges that he will not follow in their path.

In verse 5 David acknowledges that the best part of his life isn't all of God's gifts but the Giver himself. Any good thing he has not only comes from God but is sustained by God. God is the true foundation and security of all good things in our lives and we should be careful to never take that for granted.

In verse 6 he turns to think on all the good blessings God has poured out on Him. We should daily do this in prayer. Even in the hardest times we should learn to count our blessings. "Name them one by one."[1] Often if we take time to specifically thank God for specific blessings, joy and worship will rise in our hearts.

One of the most important things we can all learn to do is trace the sunbeam back to the sun.[2] Here's what I mean. Imagine if you had been born blind and were suddenly healed. The light you saw was overwhelming and beautiful to you. You saw beams of

1. Oatman, "Count Your Blessings," 563.
2. Lewis, *Letters to Malcolm*, 89–90.

sunlight pouring through a window and it thrilled your soul. Then a friend might say, "If you like the sunbeams, come and look out the window to the source." The sun itself, the source of the beams, is so big and beautiful it is truly overwhelming. In a similar way the blessings of God are lavish and wonderful. But they pale in comparison to looking fully into his face and character. Turn the eyes of your heart from the gifts to the Giver. Take time today and every day to meditate on his wonderful character as a good Father and wonderful Savior as you thank him for all his many gifts.

Verse 7 mentions an important phenomenon. As we begin to build a regular routine of prayer and meditation we will probably notice something new happening in our lives. There will be times where we aren't necessarily directly meditating on a certain passage and yet the Lord will bring it to mind. Maybe we studied it earlier that day. Maybe we memorized it years ago. But now, laying in our beds or out for a late night walk we may be processing some hardship we are going through. We may be specifically asking the Lord for wisdom or merely pouring out our thoughts to him in a more generic way. And then a passage of Scripture may rise in our minds. A new insight will form that we've never seen before. What's happening? The Lord is counseling us. You might say the Lord is "speaking" or at least illuminating his word to you in a fresh way. Be sure to slow down and pay attention!

Verse 8 refers to the idea of intentionally setting my mind on the Lord. I must be regularly purposeful to focus the eyes of my heart on eternal truth and not on passing circumstance. When we can look at Christ with our mind's eye there will be a stability and confidence the world cannot fully understand dwelling in our souls like a bedrock foundation.

This stability is something we all long for. When we experience it we will also experience deep joy that the world can't touch. Verse 9 describes this experience. Everything about David is caught up in worshipping God. Verse 10 goes deeper. Even if we are to die, we will be raised again, just as our older brother Christ was. He conquered the grave for us. What else should we fear?!

Lastly in verse 11 we see David ending in a place of great confidence and joy. He knows that God will give him all the wisdom he needs to live a godly life. Just as important He knows that God will meet him along the way and fill him with true joy. The deepest pleasures don't come from sin, not even from God's best gifts. Rather they come in the presence of the Giver himself. And these perfect pleasures will be given to his people forever in the next life!

## READ AND REMEMBER

With the above context in mind, read Psalm 16 once slowly.

## ASK AND ANSWER

Read Psalm 16 a second time jotting down any thoughts, questions, or insights here or in the margins.

## WRITE AND WORSHIP

In light of your questions and insights, as well as the context above, journal and pray through Psalm 16 below in your own words. Write out your worshipful meditation and prayer as you go. When you are done spend a few moments singing the hymn that follows whether out loud or in your mind. All the while ask the Holy Spirit to speak to you and give you fresh insight as you go.

## ON JORDAN'S STORMY BANKS

by Samuel Stennett

On Jordan's stormy banks I stand, And cast a wishful eye To Canaan's fair and happy land, Where my possessions lie.

All o'er those wide extended plains Shines one eternal day; There God the Son forever reigns And scatters night away.

No chilling winds nor pois'nous breath Can reach that healthful shore; Sickness and sorrow, pain and death Are felt and feared no more.

When shall I reach that happy place, And be forever blest? When shall I see my Father's face, And in His bosom rest?

I am bound for the promised land, I am bound for the promised land; O who will come and go with me? I am bound for the promised land.

## LISTEN AND LEARN

Spend a few extra minutes meditating on verses 5–9 in stillness.

# Day 7 Psalm 18

## CHAPTER AND CONTEXT

Psalm 18 was written later in David's life. King Saul is dead. David is ruling. Many of his enemies have been defeated. He is looking back on all the good the Lord has done for him. Psalm 18 gives us much insight into how to truly give the credit and praise to the Lord for all the benefits He has given us.

There are many dangers in the Christian life. When times are hard there's the danger of losing faith in God. But when times are good there's the danger of forgetting God and thinking that you have built a great life for yourself all by yourself. See Deuteronomy 8:10–18.

At some point when David was riding high on life he paused and looked back. He noticed that God in His sovereignty had been guiding him the whole way. He remembered his military victories but acknowledged that his true victory came because God was fighting for him behind the scenes. Are you careful to do that when blessings abound in your life? We should be.

In verses 4 through 6 it seems as though David was remembering some of his worst days and lowest moments. Why would he do that? There's something very powerful about getting to a mountain top and looking way back down in the valley where you started walking so long ago. It can powerfully stir up deep gratitude in your heart to see the pit that the Lord has delivered you from.

To have a strong and faithful prayer and worship life we must not only seek God when we are broken, desperate, and struggling. We must learn to pause and look back after the deliverance has come. We must make it a habit to slow down, look back, and then look up with praise, worship, and overflowing gratitude to the one who accomplishes all good things for me! This is what we find David doing in this psalm. He is honest about how bad things were. But he is now overwhelmingly happy for how well things are going, especially in light of his past.

Verses 7 through 15 are very interesting. David makes it sound as though God showed up in a supernatural, out of the ordinary way and fought his battles for him. David makes it sound as if God stepped out of heaven and brought hail and fire, lighting and floods to bear to wipe out David's enemies. Obviously God can do things like that if he pleases and he has done it before.

But when you read 1 Samuel you see David winning military victories. David killed Goliath with a sling and a stone, not with hail from heaven. Saul died by his own sword in a normal military battle. What is David doing? Is this mere hyperbole?

No. David is acknowledging the reality that we can't see with our physical eyes but only with the eyes of faith. God often works through the natural means and processes to accomplish his purposes in this life. If you have a friend dying from cancer who is miraculously healed you should obviously praise God. But if you have another friend dying from cancer who is healed through months of radiation at the hands of doctors and nurses *you should equally praise God*. God can work supernaturally without practical processes but more often he works through the natural processes of life to accomplish his good works. That should in no way lessen our praise of him.

The problem is that it often does lessen our praise. Often when God blesses us through some "normal" means of life we tend to forget God. We tend to take the credit for ourselves and let the glory go to our heads. We must be aggressive to fight against this through prayer, meditation, and worship.

Even our salvation so full and free came partially through very normal means. A man was nailed to a tree. He suffered, bled, and died. Through something very normal in one sense, our sin debt was paid. Yes the Lord supernaturally raised Christ from the dead. We should sing, shout, and praise God for both Christ's death on the cross and for his resurrection, all done in my place!

We should also learn in small things and big, in mundane things and the extraordinary to pause and give God praise. God gets all the credit. All good gifts come from him, regardless of how they come (James 1:17).

## READ AND REMEMBER

With the above context in mind, read Psalm 18 once slowly.

## ASK AND ANSWER

Read 2 Samuel 22 which is a slightly different version of the same psalm. Notice any differences or similarities that stand out.

## WRITE AND WORSHIP

In light of your insights, as well as the context above, journal and pray through Psalm 18 below in your own words. Write out your worshipful meditation and prayer as you go. Focus as much on praise today as you can. If you don't have time to journal in light of every verse that is ok. Do what you can. When you are done, spend a few moments singing the hymn that follows whether out loud or in your mind. All the while ask the Holy Spirit to speak to you and give you fresh insight as you go.

## MY FAITH HAS FOUND A RESTING PLACE

by Lidie H. Edmunds

My faith has found a resting place Not in device of creed: I trust the Everlasting One His wounds for me shall plead
Enough for me that Jesus saves This ends my fear and doubt; A sinful soul I come to Him He'll never cast me out.
My heart is leaning on the Word The written Word of God: Salvation by my Savior's name Salvation thru His blood.
My great Physician heals the sick The lost He came to save; For me His precious blood He shed For me His life He gave.
I need no other argument, I need no other plea; It is enough that Jesus died, And that He died for me.

## LISTEN AND LEARN

Write any final insights you have here.

# Day 8 Psalm 19

## CHAPTER AND CONTEXT

Psalm 19 is about revelation. God has made himself known to humanity. The first way that he does this is through creation. When we look into the night sky and see the stars and the moon they silently shout at us, "There is a Creator! He is great and glorious!" Creation does not give us enough information to be saved. It does give us enough data to know that God is real. He is living and active. Even a blind man feels the wind and the rain and knows God exists.

Everyone who is paying attention to reality knows there is a God. Anyone who denies his existence has no excuse. See Romans 1:18–20. Rather than argue about his existence we should bow and worship his splendor!

Even someone born blind, dumb, and deaf can know the reality of this creator. Even if they can't see the sunshine they can feel its warmth. Nothing is hidden from its heat. Nothing on planet earth survives without the life-giving heat of the sun.

In verse 6 David sings triumphantly of how the sun oversees and influences this whole planet. Then in verse 7 he starts to speak of the law of God. It can seem to be an abrupt transition at first. But in reality David is saying, as the sun gives physical insight, life, and warmth to all people on this planet, so God's word speaks to all reality on this earth. Nothing escapes the authority of God's law. All of life is influenced and governed by it.

Furthermore, as God reveals himself to humanity through creation, even more so does he reveal himself through his infallible word! God's word is complete. It gives us everything we need for life and salvation. God's word is what raises the spiritually dead and makes them alive. See Romans 10:17.

The Bible gives me all the principles of wisdom I need to live a godly life. It is sufficient for me. God's word is true. It is the key to experiencing true happiness in life! As we study God's word he will give us the insight we need to make important decisions and also the joy we need to keep us going.

God's word is absolutely true and trustworthy. If I am wise I will humble myself before this God and his word. My heart will be filled with joy and with holy reverence as I hear and obey. Knowing God should bring rejoicing to my life. But walking with this living Lord also brings a humble, trembling before him.

We should value God's word because it is the clear revelation of who he is. We should prize his word more than all the money in the world or the best food we could ever find. Do you treasure and esteem God's word like that?

To benefit from God's word the most we must take it seriously. There should be true awe in our hearts when we read the word. There should be a sense of being overwhelmed by the greatness of our God. We should take all that he says incredibly seriously. But this seriousness should not be morbid. Rather we should be trembling in worship, ecstatic with joy at all the good he has shown us and continues to show us.

In verses 13–14 David mentions two different kinds of sins. (See Numbers 15:22–31, especially verses 29–30 for more on this.) There are sins we commit that we may not even be aware of. These are sins that God in his mercy forgives in his people, even if we don't realize we have anything to confess in that moment. What a gracious Savior!

More importantly there are sins we are fully aware that we sometimes choose to do anyway. We cannot excuse these arrogant sins. We must avoid at all costs such outright, willful rebellion. If we do catch ourselves in such a moment we must repent as fast as possible. We cannot abuse God's rich mercy. It is wrong and stupid to test God's grace.

We should join David in honest humility that we aren't above any sins. We should know the sins that most easily and regularly tempt us personally (Hebrews 12:1). We should pray in advance each day that the Lord would "lead us not into temptation" (Matthew 6:13). Don't pray that generically but pray it in light of your besetting sins and the sins that most easily entangle you.

Lastly, don't end your prayer times focused on your sinfulness. That will be depressing. Rather remember that though you are a great sinner, you have a much greater Savior! End by focusing on your kinsman Redeemer! You have a spiritual big brother who bought your sinful soul out of the orphanage of this world with his very own blood. Rejoice and worship that his blood can cover all of our sin. The small hidden sins and the large presumptive sins are drowned in his blood when we turn to him in faith! Focus more on your Savior and less on your sin!

## READ AND REMEMBER

With the above context in mind, read Psalm 19 once slowly.

## ASK AND ANSWER

Read it again and jot down any questions or insights you have.

## WRITE AND WORSHIP

In light of your insights, as well as the context above, journal and pray through Psalm 19 below in your own words. Be sure to confess any sin that comes to mind. Also pray against sin you may be tempted by in the future. When you are done, spend a few moments singing the hymn that follows whether out loud or in your mind. All the while ask the Holy Spirit to speak to you and give you fresh insight as you go.

## ALL CREATURES OF OUR GOD AND KING

by St. Francis of Assisi; translated by William H. Draper

All creatures of our God and King, Lift up your voice and with us sing Alleluia, Alleluia! Thou burning sun with golden beam, Thou silver moon with softer gleam, O praise Him, O praise Him Alleluia, alleluia, alleluia! Amen.

Thou rushing wind that art so strong, Ye clouds that sail in heav'n along, O praise Him, Alleluia! Thou rising morn in praise rejoice, Ye lights of evening, find a voice, O praise Him, O praise Him, Alleluia, alleluia, alleluia! Amen.

Thou flowing water, pure and clear, Make music for thy Lord to hear, Alleluia, Alleluia! Thou fire so masterful and bright, That givest man both warmth and light, O praise Him, O praise Him, Alleluia, alleluia, alleluia! Amen.

And all ye men of tender heart, Forgiving others, take your part, O sing ye, Alleluia! Ye who long pain and sorrow bear, Praise God and on Him cast your care, O praise Him, O praise Him, Alleluia, alleluia, alleluia! Amen.

Let all things their Creator bless, And worship Him in humbleness, O praise Him, Alleluia! Praise, praise the Father, praise the Son, And praise the Spirit, Three in One, O praise Him, O praise Him, Alleluia, alleluia, alleluia! Amen.

## LISTEN AND LEARN

Write any final thoughts here.

# Day 9 Psalm 23

## CHAPTER AND CONTEXT

We don't know exactly when this psalm was written. It seems to have been written during or soon after a time of great hardship. It is the most well-known and one of the most beloved psalms. It is helpful to remember that God often uses our pain to produce true beauty and life change. Oftentimes, the places of greatest pain, weakness, and trial are turned for our best blessings, victories, and triumphs.

David begins by calling God his shepherd. Many Israelites might have spoken of God as "their" shepherd or "our" shepherd. Few would have been bold enough to call God "my" shepherd. David had experienced so much depth in his intimacy with the Lord that he felt comfortable speaking about God in very personal ways. This is a benefit that can come from learning to cling to God desperately in the midst of hardship.

For us to get the most out of our meditation on God as our shepherd we must fully embrace the fact that we are sheep. Sheep are not known for their strength, speed, wisdom, nor skill. They need a shepherd and so do we. We are sheep, but we are his sheep. We are weak and defenseless if left to ourselves. But with him, we have all we need and much more.

Many of us would be quick to say that we do believe these theological truths. But do we really? Do we live as though these things are true? Can you honestly say, "I shall not want"? Do you feel the depth and reality of the fact that the God who runs the universe orchestrates all things for your good? Can you rest in that reality when all around your soul gives way?[1] John Newton wisely said, "Everything is needful that He sends; nothing can be needful that He withholds."[2]

1. Mote, "The Solid Rock" 402.
2. Newton, *Works of John Newton*, 147.

Sheep are so timid that they often will not drink if the water is too loud or moving too fast. The good shepherd knows his fearful sheep and finds quiet waters and green pastures that minister to their deepest needs. The Lord knows us better than we know ourselves.

Have you ever meditated on the fact that one of the ten most important commandments in God's world is for his people to rest one day out of every seven? Most of us in our arrogance don't think or feel that we really need a full twenty-four hour cessation from our labors. But God knows better than us. He commands that we rest! What an amazing God! He is not a demanding dictator seeking to squeeze out of us every last ounce of work he can. No! Rather, he wants us to thrive and flourish in this life in ways that we enjoy but in ways that also honor and glorify him!

God's commitment to his own glory in your life should be fuel for your prayers. God is committed to your spiritual growth. When you are struggling, weak, and suffering, pray that God would grow you up in Christ, for his name's sake. These are prayers God will always answer. He may not answer exactly when and how we want but when we pray according to his will we will receive what we truly want at the deepest levels of our heart.

The first three verses of this psalm seem too good to be true, as though life were one constant picnic of comfort and ease. The picture painted seems like an eternal vacation but we know this is not reality. Verse 4 is a strong dose of reality. Even for the most godly saints there will be times and seasons where death seems to hang like a cloud over us. There may be times we think we are about to die. There may be times we want to die. David had experienced such hardship before.

David has no fear because God is with him. This God walks with his people with his rod in hand. He can use the rod to fight and protect us when need be. He can also use the rod to discipline us when we are out of line. Psalm 23 is not a promise that we will never suffer pain. It is a promise that God will use all the pain he brings in our lives for our good. Just like a loving parent may severely discipline a child to warn them and train them, God will do whatever it takes to protect us from sin and our own stupid decisions causing long term damage in our lives. We must trust his motives even when we doubt his methods.

Second Samuel 17 tells the story of David running for his life from his son Absalom. In the midst of this battle a friend brings food for David and his men. God is with us even in the hardest of times. He will meet the true needs of our lives. We must trust him even when the circumstances seem to say he is untrustworthy.

The word in verse 6 for "follow" could literally be translated "chase" or "pursue." God is so committed to his people in love that even when we try to run from him, he will track us down and tackle us. He won't let us leave him even if we try. The clearest example of this pursuit is Christ leaving his Father's throne above to come suffer, die, and rise for us. This should so convince us of his love that no matter what happens to us, we never doubt his commitment to us.

## READ AND REMEMBER

With the above context in mind, read Psalm 23 once slowly.

## ASK AND ANSWER

Read it again and jot down any questions or insights you have.

## WRITE AND WORSHIP

In light of your insights, as well as the context above, journal and pray through Psalm 23 below in your own words. When you are done spend a few moments singing the hymn that follows whether out loud or in your mind. All the while ask the Holy Spirit to speak to you and give you fresh insight as you go.

# I NEED THEE EVERY HOUR

by Annie S. Hawks, Robert Lowry, Refrain

I need Thee ev'ry hour, Most gracious Lord; No tender voice like Thine Can peace afford.

I need Thee ev'ry hour, Stay Thou nearby; Temptations lose their pow'r When Thou art nigh.

I need Thee ev'ry hour, In joy or pain; Come quickly, and abide, Or life is vain.

I need Thee ev'ry hour, Teach me Thy will, And Thy rich promises In me fulfill.

I need Thee, O I need Thee; Ev'ry hour I need Thee! O bless me now, my Savior, I come to Thee.

## LISTEN AND LEARN

Write any last thoughts or insights down here.

# Day 10 Psalm 25

## CHAPTER AND CONTEXT

Once again we are not sure when David wrote this psalm but it was during a time of great hardship. This psalm is a broken acrostic. Each line starts with the next letter of the Hebrew alphabet. But one line seems to be missing. This is probably intentional. It is a subtle way to tell us that God gives us all the guidance in life that we need, but it often doesn't seem that way. There are many times in life where we feel like we need more from God. We must learn to trust that he is providing all we need and yet this world is still filled with pain, hardship, and confusion. But his grace is enough to lead us through if we will persevere in faith, even when everything does not make sense to us.

Often times when we pray for wisdom, insight, and guidance our former sins may come to mind. At times our heart can accuse us. There is a sense in which we can be overwhelmed with the reality of how sinful we are and thus, left to ourselves, all we deserve from God is wrath. This isn't a good basis to go to God and ask for help.

We must remind ourselves of his great covenant love and grace. We must plead with him in prayer to interact with us not on the basis of what we deserve but on the foundation of his love and promises to us in Christ. We see David doing this in verses 4 through 9. David is pleading for help all the while remembering he doesn't deserve anything good from God. But to combat these doubts and fears he begs God to answer him not based on his character but on God's character.

God is a loving Father who loves to give great gifts to his kids. He is a covenant keeping God who makes promises to his people and then always comes through. These facts about God's nature must be the ultimate foundation of our prayer life and of our confidence. Our hope doesn't stem from our performance but from the promises of our Savior. One commentary said, "Trust . . . is neither naïve and misplaced confidence, nor is it self-confidence; it is a human response to God's self-revelation."[1]

If the Psalm ended there we might be tempted to abuse grace. There might be a sense in which God's grace and mercy is so great and good we cease to care how we respond. We are tempted to think at times, "I can keep on sinning with impunity and God will keep on blessing cause that's just what he does!" This would obviously be sinful. See Romans 6:1–2 for more on that attitude and perspective.

But this is not the message of the Bible nor of this specific psalm. God's grace and mercy is so radically good that it doesn't just forgive us, it changes us. It sanctifies us and changes us from the inside out. Notice verse 10. We are to keep his covenant. We are to obey his word. This does not mean that we are expected to live in sinless perfection which is impossible for us in this life. Rather it means that we are to take seriously the fact that if we are in Christ, we have been spiritually married to Christ. Out of our great enjoyment of and gratitude for his saving love, we should respond with worshipful obedience. What exactly does this practically look like?

It means that we repent of all known sin by the power of his indwelling Spirit. We confess our sins to him and ask for fresh mercy to cover them. We endeavor by grace to pursue new obedience in every avenue of our lives. We don't take sin lightly. We fight it with all of the might the Spirit provides.

Notice verse 11. David is not proclaiming he has arrived at sinless perfection. He still asks for forgiveness. And yet you cannot read this psalm and not get the sense that David loves God and wants to obey and please him and walk in intimacy and friendship with him. Is that your heart's desire today?

This psalm is about becoming the kind of person that God will guide into greater holiness and further insight. The goal is to become humble, broken, honest, and hungry for more of God. Is that happening to you?

Keep the eyes and hopes of your heart focused on him as your deliverer (verse 15.) Pour out all the longings, desires, and fears of your heart to him honestly in prayer (verses 16–20.) Be a person

---

1. Craigie and Tate, *Psalms 1–50*, 218.

of honesty, integrity, and wholeness waiting on God to fully and finally redeem you from all your earthly troubles (verses 21–22.)

## READ AND REMEMBER

With the above context in mind, read Psalm 25 once slowly and out loud if at all possible.

## ASK AND ANSWER

Read it again and jot down any questions or insights you have.

## WRITE AND WORSHIP

In light of your insights, as well as the context above, journal and pray through Psalm 25 below in your own words. Remind yourself of God's covenant love. When you are done, spend a few moments singing the hymn that follows whether out loud or in your mind. All the while ask the Holy Spirit to speak to you and give you fresh insight as you go.

## OUR GREAT SAVIOR

by J. Wilbur Chapman

Jesus! What a Friend for sinners! Jesus! Lover of my soul; Friends may fail me, foes assail me, He, my Savior, makes me whole.

Jesus! What a Strength in weakness! Let me hide myself in Him; Tempted, tried and sometimes failing, He, my Strength, my victory wins.

Jesus! What a Help in sorrow! While the billows o'er me roll, Even when my heart is breaking, He, my Comfort helps my soul.

Jesus! What a Guide and keeper! While the tempest still is high, Storms about me, night o'er takes me, He, my Pilot, hears my cry.

Jesus! I do now receive Him, More than all in Him I find, He hath granted me forgiveness, I am His and He is mine.

Hallelujah! What a Savior! Hallelujah! What a Friend! Saving, helping, keeping, loving, He is with me to the end.

## LISTEN AND LEARN

Write any final thoughts here.

# Day 11 Psalm 26

## CHAPTER AND CONTEXT

This psalm was written when David was being falsely accused. This is something we will all probably experience at some point in life and it is never enjoyable. When this happens to us everything in us wants to rise up and defend ourselves. But this often makes things worse. What then can we do when we are blamed for something we did not do?

The first five verses of this psalm may make us feel uncomfortable. It almost seems that David is saying, "I'm sinless! I deserve better than this." But that's not the case.

Imagine you had been accused of attempting to assassinate the president of the United States. If someone came to your house and interrogated you about the attempt, you would likely passionately defend yourself in this matter: "That's not true! There's no truth in these accusations at all! It's all lies! I've done nothing of the sort!"

In that moment you wouldn't be saying that you've never sinned in your life. You would be protesting your innocence in light of the very specific charges that had been brought against you. That's what we often find David doing in the psalms.

This psalm was likely written when David was on the run from King Saul. Saul likely had some of his followers who were saying that David had tried to usurp the throne. David had probably been accused of attempting to throw Saul from the throne. See 1 Samuel 24:9. Nothing could be further from the truth. At times David had opportunities to explain this to King Saul but those moments were few and far between. See 1 Samuel 24:10–15. But the real key to situations like this is what David says in 1 Samuel 24:15.

David and Saul seem to come to a good understanding and agreement that day. But David doesn't follow Saul back home. And it's not long before Saul is trying to kill David again. It's not wrong to try to reason with our accusers, in fact it's right. But we can't ultimately put our hope there. We must put all of our hopes and expectations in the Lord who judges all things correctly. We turn to him and plead our case. That was what we find David doing in Psalm 26.

David is passionately pleading his case before the all-knowing, all wise, all trustworthy judge of the universe: "Look into my heart, God. You know I've not plotted against Saul! I don't hate him! I'm trying to submit and be faithful!"

In verses 6 through 8 David imagines himself worshipping God at the tabernacle. He's basically saying, "At the end of the day Lord I live to please you, to honor you, to be right with you. There's no guarantee I can be put right with my enemies in this life. But by the blood of the sacrifice I can be put right with you! And that's all that really matters in this life!"

This is key when we are experiencing conflict with others in life. If we've sinned we must repent and confess and do all we can to make things right. See Romans 12:18. But we can't control the other person. We can't make them forgive us of any perceived offenses, repent of and relent of their sin and false understandings of us. Our best recourse is prayer.

Pour out your heart in prayer to God. Confess your sins but also confess your woes. Tell him of your suffering. The Lord Jesus Christ knows what it's like to be falsely accused. You will find him a very sympathetic judge.

Lastly, ask him to fight your battles for you. Ask him to vindicate you in the right way and time. Leave the matter fully in his hands. Resolve to do your part to be humble, honest and holy moving forward. But never take the whole matter into your hand. Never seek to guarantee a good result and vindication for yourself in this life all by yourself. You can't do it. Seeking to do so often causes more harm than good.

Pour out your anxieties before him and then leave them there. See 1 Peter 5:6–7. David ends Psalm 26 in verses 9 through 12 with confidence and hope but also with realism. This is not pie in the sky, everything will be easy now, fairy tale faith. It's a gritty, biblical honesty.

Say to God in prayer: "I'm going to do my part to be holy. But oh Lord, fight my battles for me. Defend me. Vindicate me!

Protect me. Keep me humble, holy, and faithful. Reconcile me to my enemies if it be your will. But mainly, keep me near unto you and I'll be happy."

## READ AND REMEMBER

With the above context in mind, read Psalm 26 once slowly.

## ASK AND ANSWER

Read it again and jot down any questions or insights you have.

## WRITE AND WORSHIP

In light of your insights, as well as the context above, journal and pray through Psalm 26 below in your own words. Pray in light of any conflicts you may currently be in with others. When you are done, spend a few moments singing the hymn that follows whether out loud or in your mind. All the while ask the Holy Spirit to speak to you and give you fresh insight as you go.

## JESUS PAID IT ALL

by Elvina M. Hall

I hear the Savior say, "Thy strength indeed is small! Child of weakness, watch and pray, Find in Me thine all in all"
Lord, now indeed I find Thy pow'r, and Thine alone, Can change the leper's spots And melt the heart of stone.
For nothing good have I Whereby Thy grace to claim I'll wash my garments white In the blood of Calv'ry's Lamb.
And when before the throne I stand in Him complete, "Jesus died my soul to save," My lips shall still repeat.
Jesus paid it all, All to Him I owe; Sin had left a crimson stain He washed it white as snow.

## LISTEN AND LEARN

Write any final thoughts or insights here.

# Day 12 Psalm 27

## CHAPTER AND CONTEXT

Sometimes it's actually helpful not to know exactly when a psalm was written. That way it's easier to apply it to whatever situation we may be facing at the time. David may have been in the midst of trouble when this psalm was written or he may have been anticipating future trouble. Either way this psalm is a great example of how to deal with the fears that can encircle our hearts.

The main issue is always to get my mind's eye more focused on Christ than it is on my present circumstances or even my hypothetical earthly circumstances. Christ is my Savior. If he has loved me enough to get me out of the greatest trouble of God's wrath through his own blood, I can be confident that he will always do what is best for me, moment by moment.

David knew that God was personally committed to him. God would give him all the insight, direction, and protection that he needs in whatever situation he faces. He starts this meditation by reminding himself of this fact. For me too, so much of a good meditation life is speaking to myself. It is reminding myself to look long and hard at reality. It is forcing myself to focus on the promises of God until the reality of them starts to burn and shine in my heart in a controlling manner.

In verse 2 David seems to look back on some hard circumstance where God had clearly fought for him and delivered him. In verse 3 David looks forward to the worst situation he can imagine and reminds himself that even then, God will be there to fight for him. There is no need to fear. God goes before us and he is our rear guard. Whom shall we fear?

John Calvin is helpful in explaining this practice: "he fortifies himself beforehand, and as it were brings together matter for confidence: for it is necessary that the saints earnestly wrestle with themselves to repel or subdue the doubts which the flesh is so prone to cherish."[1] As we see troubles potentially approach, we must have the maturity and discipline to remind ourselves of what we know to be true of our Savior and deliverer.

As David remembers God's past provision and prays for it in the future, he is probably reminded of two things. One, there is a sweet remembrance of God's nearness in times past. Secondly, there is the realization that God doesn't always protect us in hardship. Out of these twin realities verse 4 arises. This one thing I want! Yes, I would love physical protection. But even if I don't get that, what I really want is your presence, your nearness, to see you, and to worship!

Wanting and asking for God's gifts is not wrong. But above and beyond that, we should always long for God himself. Get the Giver and you've gotten everything.

As David has meditated on God's past provisions and the reality of who God is and how worthy he is, praise starts to fill his heart. We see David bursting forth with a type of newfound confidence in verses 5 and 6. This is where true meditation can lead us.

Notice that David does not stop here. Rather, in verses 7 and 9 he begins to pray even more fervently. His confidence in God leads to pushy prayer. "God I need you once again. Please come through! Don't abandon me to my enemies." This psalm is so real to our experience. It resonates with the pendulum that swings in our hearts. One minute we can be praising God with great calm confidence. The next moment, fear can creep back in. We must persevere in the place of prayer until all the knowledge we have of God sinks to the basement of our heart and builds a sure foundation of hope and confidence there.

Notice David in verse 8 essentially saying, "God, I'm doing all I know to do. I'm doing my part! I'm doing what you've told me to do! Please be faithful! Please come through! Please do your part." This is a great example of the type of clinging, desperate prayer that should fill our lives.

In verse 10 again David seems to imagine the worst case scenario. "Even if my own family abandoned me, you never will. I can trust you." Confidence is returning to fill his heart.

---

1. Calvin, *Psalms, vol. 1*, 422.

Christ was abandoned by his Father on the cross, in our place. By the eye of faith we have seen the ultimate goodness of God come down to earth for us. If God loved us enough to get us out of hell, he will ultimately get us out of all our secondary troubles. This is the confidence that we can and should daily live in. This should fill us with unspeakable courage.

## READ AND REMEMBER

With the above context in mind, read Psalm 27 once slowly.

## ASK AND ANSWER

Read it again and jot down any questions or insights you have.

## WRITE AND WORSHIP

In light of your insights, as well as the context above, journal and pray through Psalm 27 below in your own words. Pray in light of any hardships you may currently be in or any that you anticipate. When you are done, spend a few moments singing the hymn that follows whether out loud or in your mind. All the while ask the Holy Spirit to speak to you and give you fresh insight as you go.

## AT THE CROSS

by Isaac Watts,; Ralph E. Hudson, Refrain

Alas! And did my Savior bleed? And did my Sovereign die? Would
He devote that sacred head For sinners such as I!
Was it for crimes that I have done He groaned upon the tree? Amazing pity! grace unknown! And love beyond degree!
Well might the sun in darkness hide And shut His glories in, When
Christ, the mighty Maker, died For man the creature's sin.
But drops of grief can ne'er repay The debt of love I owe: Here, Lord
I give myself away- 'Tis all that I can do!
At the cross, at the cross where I first saw the light And the burden
of my heart rolled away It was there by faith I received my sight,
And now I am happy all the day!

## LISTEN AND LEARN

Write any last thoughts or insights here.

# Day 13 Psalm 32

## CHAPTER AND CONTEXT

This psalm was probably written after David's encounter with Nathan in 2 Samuel 12. David had committed adultery and murder and then covered it up for months. Nathan confronted David. David confessed and was forgiven by the Lord. This psalm is an expression of the astounding joy that is found in full and free grace and mercy.

To be blessed means to be truly happy. It means to be truly flourishing as God created you to be. All sinners are separated from this happiness to some degree because of our sin. But when we experience forgiveness, joy can return. David is not merely rejoicing in some mere legal verdict. Rather he is rejoicing in the restoration of his intimacy with God.

If someone has truly trusted in the Lord for salvation, that person can never lose salvation. See John 6:37–44, Romans 8:28–37, and Philippians 1:6. But we can lose the joy of our salvation. We can lose the experience of the benefits of that saving relationship.

When David remained hard hearted and hidden in his sin he felt cut off. His spiritual vitality dried up. God's heavy hand of conviction pressed down on him. Charles Spurgeon, the great Baptist preacher of the nineteenth century, said, "Hypocrisy is a hard game to play at, for it is one deceiver against many observers . . . Secret Sinner! If thou wantest the foretaste of damnation upon earth, continue in thy secret sins; for no man is more miserable than he who sinneth secretly, and yet trieth to preserve a character."[1]

To be forgiven is a legal verdict. It essentially means that the burden of guilt has been lifted off our shoulders and carried away. Nathan had pronounced the Lord's forgiveness on David after his simple, honest, and humble confession of sin. No penance was needed, merely brokenness and contrition.

1 Spurgeon, *Treasury vol. 1 part 1*, 291.

The first verse also mentions that David's sin had been covered. How had it been covered? David would have only known in a shadowy way that it had been covered in some sense by the blood of sacrificial animals. But even Psalm 51:16 seems to say David understood that the blood of bulls and goats wasn't the final and full answer.

For those of us in Christ living today we have a much clearer understanding of the one true Lamb of God who takes away the sin of the world. This should lead us to an even deeper sense of assurance and rest. Furthermore it should usher in a greater sense of blessedness and joy!

We have sinned. But if we trust in Christ God doesn't credit the debt of sin to our account. Rather He credits the sinlessly pure righteousness of Christ to our account. He asks that we humbly acknowledge our sin and receive his gift. He doesn't want us to try to cover our sins with our own good works or with our lies. He wants us to admit our desperate need and rest in the finished work of his Son!

When a true believer sins willfully and then tries to hide it, there will often be painful consequences. The guilt and shame will often manifest itself physically, mentally, and emotionally. This may be a bad case of ulcers or full blown depression. (There can be other, more innocent reasons for such conditions as well.) It's never good to keep quiet about our sin. At minimum we must confess to Christ our great high priest. But typically the best way to make sure that we are being honest with God and with ourselves about our sin is to be honest with someone else we must look in the eyes. David's true confession to God came as he confessed to Nathan.

As soon as we realize we have sinned; as soon as conviction sets in, we should stop sinning. We should immediately turn, repent, confess, and cry out to God in prayer. Don't hesitate for a second. Don't give sin a foothold in your life. Don't let sinful shame creep in and drive you from your loving Father. Run to him quickly in prayer and throw yourself at his great mercy. Hide in him from the wrath to come.

Remain in him. Abide in him. See John 15:5. Listen to his voice through the Scripture. Ask for wisdom on how to be holy, how to fight sin, and how to remain pure. True repentance and confession are not just about getting grace to forgive and cover my past sin. It must be about getting grace to prepare me and strengthen me to fight future temptation.

We must lay aside our stubborn ways. We must consider the dreadful end of persevering in sin. We must remind ourselves that true joy is found in Christ, never in sin.

## READ AND REMEMBER

Read Psalm 32 with the above context in mind.

## ASK AND ANSWER

Read Psalm 32 again slowly. Jot down any thoughts or insights you have.

## WRITE AND WORSHIP

Take each verse of Psalm 32 and turn it into a personal prayer, confession, or praise. Essentially, write out the whole psalm in your own words. Write it as your own, not as David's. Write it in light of your present day sin struggles. If there is any sin that you need to confess to the Lord do so here. When you are done, spend time singing the song below.

## AMAZING GRACE

by John Newton; John P. Rees, stanza 5

Amazing grace! How sweet the sound That saved a wretch like me!
I once was lost but now am found, Was blind but now I see.
'Twas grace that taught my heart to fear, And grace my fears relieved; How precious did that grace appear The hour I first believed.
The Lord has promised good to me, His word my hope secures; He will my shield and portion be As long as life endures.
Thru many dangers, toils and snares, I have already come; 'Tis grace hath brought me safe thus far, And grace will lead me home.
When we've been there ten thousand years, Bright shining as the sun, We've no less days to sing God's praise Than when we'd first begun.

## LISTEN AND LEARN

Write any final thoughts or insights or feelings of joy or thanksgiving here.

# Day 14 Psalm 34

## CHAPTER AND CONTEXT

First Samuel 21:10–15 gives us the background for this psalm. Saul is persecuting David. David runs to Israel's enemy, the Philistines, hoping to find safety there. But he is recognized and fears he might be imprisoned or killed. So, he begins to literally act like he's a crazy man who's lost his mind. Through this subterfuge he escapes.

This psalm is much less of a prayer and much more of a meditation. It is filled with praise to God but also with calls to others to trust God, obey God, and worship him as well. It is worship that leads to meditation that leads to exhortation.

David begins overwhelmed with joy in the Lord for his deliverance. He is careful to give God all the glory. It may have been easy to boast in his own wisdom or quick thinking but rather he boasts in the Lord. Even when we make wise decisions in life that turn out well, we should be quick to pause and give God the credit for working in and through us to bring about the good results that only he can guarantee.

David knew that in his leadership position, as he was faithful to praise the Lord, others would hear and join him. This should be a desire of all of us. We may not have as much influence as David. But wherever we have influence, at home, at work, or with family we should seek to leverage it for the Lord.

In verses 4 through 6 David begins to look back and remember all the faithfulness of the Lord. It is such a good thing to remind ourselves of our own history. More importantly, we can remind ourselves of the unique and specific ways God has come through for us. When we feel like we are between a rock and a hard place, looking back can give us confidence as we look ahead.

In verse 7 David is meditating on the fact that God's personal presence encamps around and surrounds his people. Nothing can touch us that has not passed through his wise, loving hands. David then bursts out in worshipful exhortation. He is passionate for as many as possible to experience God in this way.

It is likely in verse 8 he anticipates someone saying, "Well I don't know God in that way. I've not experienced such deliverance." There are at least two ways to respond to such an objection. Maybe that person has never really fully trusted in God as their savior. Maybe they go through the motions externally but have never internally rested in his work on their behalf. Is that true of you?

Secondly, there may be true believers who have simply never slowed down enough to meditate on the goodness of God adequately. I fear many of us fall into this category. The near miss with the Philistines probably happened so fast David hardly had time to meditate and worship in the midst of it. It seems he barely escaped.

This psalm is an alphabetic acrostic, meaning that each line starts with the next letter of the Hebrew alphabet. This also means this psalm probably wasn't written quickly off the cuff. David had to set aside time after the speedy deliverance to intentionally think, pray, and meditate. As he did, this psalm of worship emerged.

There is an important principle for us to glean. One of the most important things we can do in our daily time alone with the Lord is slow down and think. It's so helpful to look back over the events of the last 24 hours and intentionally remember how the Lord came through for us. We must be purposeful about our rejoicing and worship! Haphazard praise alone won't take us far. Remind yourself how you have "proved Him o'er and o'er"[1] in your own personal life.

If we really want to have the experience of tasting and seeing God with the eyes of our heart and the taste buds of our souls it will take time, effort, and intentionality. We must set aside time to slow down and purposefully recount to ourselves and to others at times, specifically how God has been good to us. This is where true praise and worship starts to grow and thrive. In the soil of intentional prayer and meditation, true experience of God's presence is sure to eventually flourish!

When we truly take time to tremble in awe before him, we will lack no good thing. We will suffer in this life. But we will have the

---

1. Stead, "'Tis So Sweet," 350.

better and deeper benefits of spiritual blessings in our soul, which should be our true desires. Take extra time today if you can to read and meditate on the quotes that follow.

Kidner says that this meditation should be "more than a casual sampling."[2] John Calvin agrees: "the Psalmist indirectly reproves men for their dullness in not perceiving the goodness of God, which ought to be to them more than a matter of simple knowledge . . . they devour the gifts of God without relishing them . . . He . . . calls upon them to stir up their senses, and to bring a palate endued with some capacity of tasting, that God's goodness may become known to them . . . be made manifest to them . . . there is nothing on the part of God to prevent the godly . . . from arriving at the knowledge of his goodness by actual experience."[3]

John Gil, the old Baptist commentator, teaches that God gives us an "experimental knowledge of the grace and goodness of God in Christ . . . in such manner as to live upon it, and be nourished by it; and though this is not a superficial taste of things, nor a single one only, being frequently repeated . . . and every taste now influences and engages trust in the Lord,"[4] Matthew Poole, another older commentator, adds that we should "consider it seriously and thoroughly and affectionately . . . This is opposed to those slight and vanishing thoughts which men have of it."[5]

## READ AND REMEMBER

With the above context in mind, read Psalm 34 slowly.

## ASK AND ANSWER

Read Psalm 34 again jotting down any questions or answers you have.

2. Kidner, *Psalms* 1–72, 158.
3. Calvin, *Psalms vol. 1*, 521–2.
4. Gil, *Psalms*, 377.
5. Poole, *Commentary vol. 2*, 52.

## WRITE AND WORSHIP

Read, pray and meditate through Psalm 34. As you do, write out your own meditation and worship as you go. Try to think of specific times that God has come through for you. Take time to meditate so that hopefully the goodness of God will burn and shine in your heart and lead you to true worship. When you are done, spend time meditating on the hymn below.

## LEANING ON THE EVERLASTING ARMS

by Elisha A. Hoffman

What a fellowship, what a joy divine, Leaning on the everlasting arms; What a blessedness, what a peace is mine, Leaning on the everlasting arms.

O how sweet to walk in this pilgrim way, Leaning on the everlasting arms; O, how bright the path grows from day to day, Leaning on the everlasting arms.

What have I to dread, what have I to fear, Leaning on the everlasting arms? I have blessed peace with my Lord so near, Leaning on the everlasting arms.

Leaning, leaning, Safe and secure from all alarms; Leaning, leaning, Leaning on the everlasting arms.

Leaning, leaning, Safe and secure from all alarms; Leaning, leaning, Leaning on the everlasting arms.

## LISTEN AND LEARN

Write any final thoughts here.

# Day 15 Psalm 37

## CHAPTER AND CONTEXT

There's no prayer in this psalm. The entire thing is a meditation. It is also an alphabetic acrostic. This was probably done to help with memorization. One of the best reasons to memorize is that it forces you to slow down and go over the same material over and over again. Doing this often forces you to meditate whether you plan to or not. You naturally start to notice new things, make connections you wouldn't have otherwise seen, and ask more questions. This can lead to deeper insight as well as intimacy.

Another feature in this psalm is that there are three main themes that come out clearly in the first eleven verses. They are then repeated throughout the psalm. This is another way that this psalm helps with meditation.

In some ways this psalm is an anti-worry psalm. The over-arching theme seems to be "Don't worry but rather . . . " Let's look at the strategies and the wisdom this psalm provides to help us in our fight against worry.

Much of the worry in our lives comes from envy. We look around and see others doing better than us and we are jealous. This is exceedingly hard when we feel that prominent sinners seem to thrive and saints seem to suffer. David offers very simple advice. Trust the Lord.

Trusting in the Lord can seem so basic and simple we're not even sure how to evaluate if we are truly doing it. Is just declaring "I trust God" enough? Is it a certain feeling? David gives us the answer in verse 3. If you truly trust your doctor, then you'll follow the prescriptions he gives you. If you truly trust the Lord you will obey Him. You will do good.

Then comes a powerful phrase that has been variously trans-lated; "dwell in the land and befriend faithfulness." Here is my best understanding of what this means: Focus on faithfulness, God's and yours. Focus on how faithful God has been to you, all the goodness he has provided and continues to provide. Enjoy God and delight in his great gifts. When you do that the only proper response is then to focus on your own faithfulness to God. Live faithfully. Live humbly. Live obediently. Be happy and content with all God is and with all he has and is doing for you. Out of the overflow of that joy live a life of holiness to honor him. Spurgeon teaches that feeding on God's faithfulness "banishes forever the hungry heart-burnings of envy."[1]

The second theme flows naturally from this. Delight in the Lord. It is not enough just to trust him. This trust must be accompanied with great joy. God promises to give us all that is best for us. He obviously doesn't grant every casual wish we ever have and certainly not our sinful ones. But he will meet the deepest desires of our hearts in his own way and timing, often in ways we could have never imagined.

One key to truly delighting ourselves in the Lord is to intentionally take our affections off of sin and lesser things and intentionally place them on the Lord. Pray for help to do this. In the place of prayer, meditate on God's goodness until your heart slowly starts to warm with a deeper delight in him alone than in all of his gifts put together.

This naturally leads to the third theme. Rest in the Lord. Verse 5 tells us to commit to obedience. Then there is a promise. In the Hebrew it literally says, "he will do." It doesn't tell us exactly what he will do. God is promising us that he will act for us. He will do what is best. He will not be passive.

Even before we were born God acted by sending Christ to die for us. He secured our salvation. He is an active God. He sees and understands our problems even better than we do. He is already acting on our behalf. Trust him. Enjoy him. Rest in him.

John Calvin is helpful:

> [I]f we stay our minds wholly upon God, instead of allowing our imaginations like others to roam after idle and frivolous fancies, all other things will be bestowed upon us in due season . . . the faithful truly feel and understand that this promise is not made to them in vain,

1 Spurgeon, *Treasury vol. 1 part 2,* 171.

since, having fixed the anchor of their faith in God, they pass their life every day in peace, while God makes it manifest in their experience, that the shadow of his hand is sufficient to protect them . . . although God may not bestow upon us what is necessary for our gratification, yet, unless our own ingratitude prevent us, we shall experience, even in famine and want, that he nourishes us graciously and liberally[2]

## READ AND REMEMBER

With the above context in mind, read Psalm 37 slowly.

## ASK AND ANSWER

Read Psalm 37:1–11 again jotting down any questions or answers you have.

## WRITE AND WORSHIP

Read, pray and meditate through Psalm 37. As you do, write out your own meditation and worship as you go. Confess any fears or worries you have. Meditate on the three themes of trusting God, enjoying God, and resting in God. If you are pressed for time, just journal on the first 11 verses today. When you are done, spend time meditating on the hymn below.

2. Calvin, *Psalms vol. 1*, 569, 573–4, 581.

## PRAISE TO THE LORD, THE ALMIGHTY

by Joachim Neander; translated by Catherine Winkworth

Praise to the Lord, the Almighty, the King of creation! O my soul, praise Him, for He is thy health and salvation! All ye who hear, Now to His temple draw near; Join me in glad adoration!

Praise to the Lord, who o'er all things so wondrously reigneth, Shelters thee under His wings, yes, so gently sustaineth! Hast thou not seen How all thy longings have been Granted in what He ordaineth?

Praise to the Lord, who doth prosper they work and defend thee; Surely His goodness and mercy here daily attend thee. Ponder anew What the Almighty can do, If with His love He befriend thee.

Praise to the Lord! O let all that is in me adore Him! All that hath life and breath, come now with praises before Him. Let the Amen Sound from His people again: Gladly for aye we adore Him. Amen.

## LISTEN AND LEARN

Write any final thoughts here.

# Day 16 Psalm 46

## CHAPTER AND CONTEXT

We do not know exactly when Psalm 46 was written. It seems to be written when Jerusalem was under siege. Second Kings 19:35 seems to be the most likely scenario. The Assyrians surrounded the city bent on conquering it. King Hezekiah looked to the Lord in prayer. God answered and sent an angel one night to kill 185,000 of the enemy troops. The siege was instantly over.

God is our true hiding place. He is our hope. He is our offense and our defense. He goes before us and behind us and is a shield all around us. He is "a very present help in trouble." He is always near. He is always ready to help. He is eager to help. He loves to rush to our aid when we call to him.

There may be times when we pray and we do not feel that he is near. There may be times when we cry out and we do not see him instantly answer as we think he should. But we must remember. On the cross, Christ got abandoned by the Father. Christ cried out on the cross and the Father was silent in wrath. Christ did not deserve that. We do deserve God's silence.

When we place our faith in Christ we can and should have utter confidence that God the Father always hears us. He always cares. He always rushes to our aid even if we do not see or experience it. That is the promise of the cross and resurrection. Jesus Christ got all the wrath we deserve. Now, in him, we get all the answered prayer he deserves.

When it seems God does not answer or is slow to answer we must remind ourselves that God is often working behind the scenes for us. Romans 8:28 promises that although all things are not good, God will work all those evil things together in the long run to coordinate for our best.

This should lead us to never quake in fear. Even if the whole world seems to crumble around us our foundation is true, sure, and unshakable. Our foundation and confidence is the Lord God, the Creator of heaven and earth.

Verse 4 speaks of the stream that makes glad the city of God. Water is a necessary resource. Few things are more necessary. But God is an even more fundamental resource for our lives. Our souls truly can't live without the breath of God. This is one reason we must daily connect with Christ through prayer.

When we regularly spend time praying and meditating on God's word, we are reminded of God's presence and nearness. He loves us. He is married to his people. If we suffer, he suffers with us, in our midst. Remember what Jesus said to Saul. He didn't say, "why do you persecute my people?" (Although He could have said that.) He said, "why are you persecuting me?" See Acts 9:4. Jesus takes our suffering personally. He experiences it with us. That's how closely he has aligned himself with us. He lives in us!

As we saw in Psalm 2 even if the whole world literally aligned itself against us, if we stand with Christ, we are in the majority. We have nothing to fear. If God is for us, who can be against us?! See Romans 8:31.

In verse 10 God essentially says, "Be quiet. Hush your crying little children. I've got this. Relax. I'm going to put the team on my back and win the victory for us, just like I always do!"

We have a part to play. But ours is the minor part. God's part is ultimately the only part that matters and the part that will win the day. Commentators argue about whether this psalm was written during a siege or after. At times it seems that the author is still in the midst of hardship. At other times, it seems the hardship is past. Even if we are in the midst of our worst suffering we should have the confidence as if it was already over; for it soon will be.

Twice this psalm mentions the God of Jacob. Jacob was a sinful and fearful man but God made a covenant with him and thus took care of him. We have an even better covenant, signed with the blood of his Son. Be still. Know him. Experience him as your God today!

## READ AND REMEMBER

Read Psalm 46 with the above context in mind.

## ASK AND ANSWER

Read Psalm 46 again slowly. Jot down any thoughts or insights you have.

## WRITE AND WORSHIP

Take each verse of Psalm 46 and turn it into a personal prayer or praise. Write out the whole psalm in your own words. Write it in light of your present day fears, worries, and concerns. When you are done, spend time singing the song below.

## A MIGHTY FORTRESS IS OUR GOD

by Martin Luther; translated by Frederick H. Hedge

A mighty fortress is our God, A bulwark never failing; Our helper he amid the flood Of mortal ills prevailing. For still our ancient foe Doth seek to work us woe His craft and pow'r are great, And, armed with cruel hate, On earth is not his equal.

Did we in our own strength confide, Our striving would be losing, Were not the right man on our side, The man of God's own choosing. Dost ask who that may be? Christ Jesus, it is He Lord Sabaoth His name, From age to age the same, And He must win the battle.

And tho this world, with devils filled, Should threaten to undo us, We will not fear, for God hath willed His truth to triumph thru us. The prince of darkness grim, We tremble not for him-His rage we can endure, For lo, his doom is sure: One little word shall fell him.

That word above all earthly pow'rs, No thanks to them, abideth; The Spirit and the gifts are ours Thru Him who with us sideth. Let goods and kindred go, This mortal life also The body they may kill; God's truth abideth still: His kingdom is forever. A-men.

## LISTEN AND LEARN

Write any final thoughts or insights here.

# Day 17 Psalm 51

## CHAPTER AND CONTEXT

Psalm 51 is one of the most well-known Psalms. The title tells us that it was written after David's sin with Bathsheba. It also tells us it was written after Nathan had confronted him which makes it even more interesting. Nathan confronted David with his sin in 2 Samuel 12:1–12. David immediately confesses his sin in verse 13. Nathan, speaking on God's behalf immediately pronounces God's forgiveness on David. There will be consequences though. David's infant child becomes sick and eventually dies. David spends the next week in prayer. It is likely during this time or sometime shortly after that he writes this psalm.

What's important to us in understanding this chronology is that David had been clearly forgiven and yet he still didn't feel forgiven. Nathan was God's mouth piece. Nathan said, "The Lord also has put away your sin; you shall not die." (2 Samuel 12:13) If we are in Christ and understand the gospel we know that we are fully forgiven for all our sins, and yet we still often feel guilty for sin in our relationship with the Lord. We may fully know and believe that we are legally forgiven in the cosmic courtroom of the universe. But when with our heavenly Father in prayer we may feel the weight of the grief that we've brought to his heart and thus feel distant from him. This psalm is for us.

Notice in verse 1 as David begs for God's mercy to blot out his transgressions he doesn't plead his sincerity. He is not trying to pay emotional penance. He's not saying, "I'm so sorry and that's why you should forgive me!" No, he begs that God would have mercy "according to your steadfast love." That's his only hope. And it's our only hope. But what a hope it is.

It is God's nature to be merciful. God likes to be gracious. God enjoys forgiving his people. Martin Luther supposedly said that wrath is God's "strange work." God will show wrath but he takes no pleasure in it. See Lamentations 3:32–33, Ezekiel 18:23, and

33:11. No matter what you've done, run to God in Christ and beg mercy based on the basis of his character, not on the strength of your repentance!

Notice in verse 4 David says, "Against you, you only, have I sinned." This isn't literally true. He sinned against many people including Uriah whom he had killed! But this is poetic language where David expresses the deepest feelings of his heart. As evil as murder is, what's ultimately so bad about sin isn't the human damage we cause but the fact that we sin against God's grace, mercy, and goodness. God has loved us so perfectly and yet we continually break his heart. This should grieve us to no end. The further down in brokenness over sin we will go, the higher up in worship for grace we will eventually go.

Verse 5 is so important because David is tracing his sin to his root. He's essentially saying, "This is who I am apart from God's grace! This wasn't a fluke. At heart I'm a murderer and an adulterer. I shouldn't even be shocked I did this in some sense!" See how these themes come out in Matthew 5:21–30 and Romans 3:9–20. We shouldn't just confess our sin but our sinfulness! Confess the root not just the fruit.

In verse 6 David acknowledges that God doesn't only want right behavior. He wants right thinking and feeling all the way in the depth of our beings! We are unable to produce this alone. Unless God shows up and cleanses us, changes us, and sustains us we have no hope. We are utterly, desperately, dependent on him, his grace, goodness, and promises to us in Christ.

Verse 8 and 12 show us the theme of this psalm again in a fresh way. David wants to feel forgiven. He wants to experience closeness to God. He wants joy to overflow from his heart as he relishes his salvation again!

Notice that verses 13 through 19 are filled with prayers and commitments to teach others of God's grace, to sing of his love, and to even see a revival of God's people in the holy city. When we have really repented in joy and experienced God's grace afresh we will want to sing, to dance, to shout, and tell others of his marvelous grace! We won't be able to keep it to ourselves. Tim Keller said the acid test of true repentance is if it attracts others because it is so joyful.[1]

The more we will be honest with ourselves, with others, and most importantly with God about our sin, the more we will see the depth of our need for Christ. Then when we turn to look at Christ anew again, it'll be like seeing him for the first time. Our joy in salvation and the gospel will be renewed, almost as if we had been saved all over again! Hallelujah! What a Savior!

## READ AND REMEMBER

In light of the above context, read Psalm 51 slowly.

## ASK AND ANSWER

Read the whole psalm again. Jot down any thoughts or questions you have.

## WRITE AND WORSHIP

Write a version of Psalm 51 in your own words. Use Psalm 51 as an outline. Confess your sins as clearly as possible. Beg mercy based on God's character not your own. Think about the mercy you have in Christ. Rejoice in your salvation afresh! Pledge yourself to new obedience. Then sing the hymn below.

1. Keller, *Praying with the Psalms*, 64.

## ALAS! AND DID MY SAVIOR BLEED?

by Isaac Watts

Alas! And did my Savior bleed And did my Sovereign die? Would He devote that sacred Head For sinners such as I?

Was it for sins that I have done He suffered on the tree? Amazing pity! Grace unknown! And love beyond degree!

Well might the sun in darkness hide And shut His glories in, When Christ, the great Redeemer, died For man the creature's sin.

Thus might I hide my blushing face While His dear cross appears, Dissolve my heart in thankfulness, And melt mine eyes to tears.

But drops of grief can ne'er repay The debt of love I owe; Here, Lord, I give myself away 'Tis all that I can do.

## LISTEN AND LEARN

Spend extra time meditating on the fourth stanza of the hymn. Write any final thoughts here.

# Day 18 Psalm 52

One of the realities we all must wrestle with each day is, "What or who is primarily influencing me today?" There are some people who don't really know God's word and thus aren't influenced by it very much at all. But there are many others who may know it very well and yet still not be influenced by it near enough. Why is that?

First Samuel 21–22 tells the story of David fleeing from Saul. He stops off to see the priest Ahimelech. David doesn't tell Ahimelech he is running from Saul. He does ask Ahimelech to provide supplies for him and his men which the priest is happy to do. Doeg was one of Saul's henchmen. He witnesses this encounter. He later tells Saul what Ahimelech has done and makes it seem as though Ahimelech was conspiring with David against Saul. Because of this Saul orders Ahimelech and his family killed and Doeg happily carries out the execution. When this tragic news comes to David he writes Psalm 52.

So much of King Saul's sin flowed from the fact that he didn't slow down and think deeply about who God was, what God wanted, and what God was doing. Rather, he was more consumed with himself. He was consumed with how others viewed him and what they thought of him. Their thoughts, words, and actions were the determining factor in how he thought, felt, and acted and this led him into much fear, sin, and rash action. The same can happen to us. We can be far too worried about what others think, say, and feel about us. Rather than being controlled by the thoughts of other humans around us, we should be controlled by the word of God. But that doesn't come naturally. We must work in conjunction with the Holy Spirit through the word and prayer to make sure we are more influenced by the word of God than by the words of men. That is what we see David doing in this psalm.

David sees how Saul and Doeg are influenced by deceptive words. He also sees how they use their own evil words to sinfully influence others. He doesn't want to be like them. They are hoping in their own cunning, wisdom, and might. David is hoping in the love, wisdom, and strength of the Lord. He is looking away from himself and his overwhelming circumstances to the God of covenant love who has pledged to save and protect him. We must learn to daily do the same.

David has been anointed to be king by the prophet. He can tell Saul has gone crazy and is influenced by a demon. It was a real temptation for him to take matters into his own hands in a sinful fashion, kill Saul, and make himself king instantly. We often face temptations to take matters into our own hands rather than patiently waiting for God's timing. We are often in a hurry which can be a sign of our weak faith. David is content to wait on God's timing and ways. Are you? Where in life are you tempted to take control in sinful and manipulative ways? Confess them today in prayer.

In verses 2 through 4 David looks at the threats of these evil men with his mind's eye. He considers them. Then in verse 5 he turns to remember the Lord and his power. He is comforted when he considers the end of all things. In verse 6 he says he is able to laugh in confidence because he knows he will have the final victory, even if he can't fully see it yet.

Everyone is hoping in something. You either hope in God and his love for you or you hope in the strength of man. You may hope in your own abilities or those of a friend or benefactor. But all human hopes are ultimately hollow ones. Paul David Tripp, a counselor and author, writes the following:

> When you look horizontally for your sense of self . . . you are all too attentive to the opinions, responses, reactions and situations around you. You look too intently at how people are responding to you, and you listen too carefully to what people are saying and how they say it. You notice discussions or plans that included you. You are troubled by the advancement of others and quietly envious of their . . . success . . . Your hyperattentiveness crushes your peace of heart, leaving worry, concern, anxiety, and/or fear in its place. It is a vicious cycle, because the more you pay

attention, the more you find reason to be concerned, and the more you're concerned, the more you pay attention . . . When you look horizontally for what you have already been given vertically, the things you look to will always fail you.[1]

Olive trees can live for many years. David reminds himself that he will live eternally in God's house. He knows that his time and his reign will surpass that of Saul and Doeg because of the promise of God.

In verse 9 David speaks in the prophetic perfect, "because you have done it." God hasn't established David as king just yet. But God has promised to. And God's word about something in the future is fully trustworthy. It is as good as done. It is solid, true, and trustworthy. We can give him praise now for the accomplishments that will come tomorrow. This is our ultimate hope. This is our salvation. This should be the reality that influences us more than anything else.

## READ AND REMEMBER

Read Psalm 52 once slowly.

## ASK AND ANSWER

Read it again and jot down any thoughts or insights you have.

## WRITE AND WORSHIP

Journal through Psalm 52. Write it out in your own words based on your own circumstances. Confess anywhere you are tempted to be more influenced by sinful men than by the word of God. Seek to take the thoughts of your heart off of your fears and place them

1. Tripp, *Lead,* 168–9.

onto the rock solid foundation of the word of God. Focus on God's goodness rather than your hardships. Sing the hymn at the end either in your mind or out loud.

## BENEATH THE CROSS OF JESUS

by Elizabeth C. Clephane

Beneath the cross of Jesus I fain would take my stand The shadow of a mighty Rock Within a weary land; A home within the wilderness, A rest upon the way, From the burning of the noontide heat, And the burden of the day.

Upon the cross of Jesus Mine eye at times can see The very dying form of One Who suffered there for me And from my smitten heart with tears Two wonders I confess The wonders of redeeming love And my unworthiness.

I take, O cross thy shadow For my abiding place; I ask no other sunshine than The sunshine of His face; Content to let the world go by, To know no gain nor loss, My sinful self my only shame, My glory all the cross.

## LISTEN AND LEARN

Write any final thoughts or impressions here.

# Day 19 Psalm 56

## CHAPTER AND CONTEXT

The background for this Psalm is the same as that of Psalm 34 that we looked at on day 14. This seems to be a record of what David thought and prayed when he was in the midst of the conflict. He runs from Saul to the Philistines hoping to find safe quarters there. Some of the Philistines recognize him and seize him. In the midst of the panic he inwardly prays. He cries out to God for deliverance. This doesn't stop him from using his wits to devise a plan to be free. But we see an important principle here. God has given us a brain and a body and we should use them to solve problems that we face. As long as we're not in sin we should move forward and try to be faithful in hardship. But all the while we should never ultimately depend on or hope in our own efforts. Even as we think and act, we should inwardly be looking away from ourselves and to our God who can guarantee deliverance.

As we act outwardly, inwardly we are depending on God to bless our efforts and make them fruitful. Notice in verse 1 that David does not plead his merit. He doesn't say, "I deserve blessings! You owe me!" Rather, he asks for grace. He does plead his neediness though. He's honest with God about the pains he has suffered and the weariness in his heart. God is drawn to help us in our sufferings!

In verses 3 and 4 we see David meditating. He is preaching truth to himself. He is reminding himself of the only sure method of deliverance. Don't pretend you're not afraid. Be honest about it! Tell the Lord how you feel. He already knows. But don't sit in your fears alone. Don't wallow in panic. Don't stare at your feelings and be consumed by them. Look up to a heavenly Father who is simultaneously compassionate and tender but is also strong, mighty, and able to save!

When we come to Christ as Savior we must remember that he is fully human as we are. We come to a great high priest who is able to sympathize with all of our weaknesses and temptations.

He really does understand. (See Hebrews 2:17–18 and 4:13–16.) But he is also fully God. He knows, understands, and controls all. He promises to orchestrate all things to work together for our best. There is such joy and hope in meditating on his power even in the midst of our worst sufferings!

In verses 5 and 6 David pours out his worries, sorrows, and complaints. He's brutally honest with God about the pain he feels. In verse 7 he pours out his anger. He asks for God to arise in anger and wipe out his enemies as we've seen him do before. As he pours out all of his negative emotions before the Lord something wonderful happens. Hope arises.

In verse 8 David is comforted. He is hopeful. He is meditating on the character of God. Imagine that you were being chased by a thief with a knife who was trying to rob you. As you run around the corner you see a police officer with a gun. You begin to yell and scream to the officer to help you. As he looks at you and listens, your confidence would start to rise. Your thoughts would begin to shift from the trouble you were in to the more powerful, well-armed, protector in front of you, who is now moving to help you.

When we persevere in meditation and prayer something similar can happen for us. As we focus our thoughts honestly more on God's character than our circumstances, hope will arise. I'm not saying we should stick our heads in the sand and pretend problems don't exist. No. Rather we should be fully honest with our compassionate God in heaven about all that we think or feel. Even when we know our thoughts and feelings probably aren't 100 percent accurate, there is something therapeutic about pouring out our heart to God in prayer, getting our eyes onto His power, and then leaving our concerns with him.

In verse 8 David remembers the Lord's compassion. In verse 9 he meditates on God's strength and on God's commitment to him personally. David's enemies pale in comparison. Even if the entire Philistine army comes after him, they are no match for the Lord!

In verses 10 and 11 he returns to his previous meditation. A large part of good meditation is repetition. Keep going back to the truths that help and impact you the most!

David ends the Psalm the way most of our prayers should ideally end. "God, you've been so good to me, that I want to live my whole life as a way to say thank you to you." Meditate on God's goodness until you *feel* relief from your problems. Then pledge to live faithfully in the future for his glory and your joy.

## READ AND REMEMBER

Read Psalm 56 slowly with the above context in mind.

## ASK AND ANSWER

Read it again and jot down any thoughts or questions you have.

## WRITE AND WORSHIP

Write out Psalm 56 in your own words. What are you struggling with right now? Pour out all of your negative emotions to the Lord in prayer. Be honest about all your pain, fear, anger, and worry. But also ask him for help. Look at his character with your mind's eye. Rest in his faithfulness. Pledge to walk in new obedience as you honor him. Finish by meditating on the hymn below.

# AND CAN IT BE?

by Charles Wesley

And can it be that I should gain An int'rest in the Savior's blood? Died He for me, who caused His pain? For me, who Him to death pursued? Amazing love! How can it be That Thou my God shouldst die for me?

He left His Father's throne above, So free, so infinite His grace! Emptied Himself of all but love, And bled for Adam's helpless race! 'Tis mercy all immense and free, For, O my God, it found out me.

Long my imprisoned spirit lay Fast bound in sin and nature's night. Thine eye diffused a quick'ning ray: I woke- the dungeon flamed with light! My chains fell off, my heart was free, I rose, went forth, and followed Thee.

No condemnation now I dread: Jesus, and all in Him, is mine! Alive in Him, my living Head, And clothed in righteousness divine, Bold I approach th' eternal throne, And claim the crown, thru Christ my own.

Amazing love! How can it be That Thou, my God, shouldst die for me!

## LISTEN AND LEARN

Write any final thoughts here.

# Day 20 Psalm 57

## CHAPTER AND CONTEXT

David ran from Saul to the Philistines but he couldn't hide there. They recognized him and wanted to arrest him. So he runs to the wilderness and hides in a cave. Saul comes to chase him with thousands of men. David has a few hundred. He must have felt overwhelmed, out-numbered, and scared.

At one point Saul camps outside of David's cave and even comes in to relieve himself. David could've easily killed the king in the dark of the cave. His men urged him to. Yet he resisted. Why?

Psalm 57 was written during those days. All of us need to hide somewhere. In Genesis 3 when Adam and Eve sinned they instantly felt shame, fear, and insecurity. They attempted to hide from each other, from God, and even from themselves. They used fig leaves, trees, blame shifting, and excuses. Our attempts to hide may be slightly more sophisticated but we all still feel the inner urge to run and hide at different times for different reasons.

Sometimes we are overwhelmed with a sense of our sin, guilt, and shame. Other times hard circumstances drive us to a place of fear, worry, and doubt. Sometimes we may just be sick and disgusted with ourselves and trying to hide from reality. But the truth remains, at different times, in different ways we are all seeking to hide from something. This isn't necessarily wrong.

We are all sinners living in a fallen, broken, sinful world. There's a lot of pain and hardship. If there are practical things we can do to ease the pain, it is right to do so as long as those practical steps don't lead us into sin.

It wasn't wrong for David to run from a crazy king and hide in a cave. It would've been wrong for David to kill Saul. He knew the difference and lived in light of the difference because in actuality he was really hiding in and hoping in God to deliver him.

Notice what David says in verse 1: "Be merciful to me, O God, for in you my soul takes refuge." Essentially he says, "I'm doing my best Lord. I'm doing my part. I'm running and hiding in this cave but it's not enough. Even here Saul follows me. But I won't kill him. My hope is not ultimately in my own efforts. My hope is in you! Actually I'm hiding in you. You are my safety and hope; not this cave, not my own efforts."

This is a huge part of godly living. Do all you can to better and improve your life without sinning. But never rest in those efforts. Look past your efforts to the words, the promises, and the character of God. Lloyd-Jones teaches, "if you can improve your circumstances by fair and legitimate means, do so, and if you cannot, and if you have to remain in a trying and difficult position, do not be mastered by it, do not let it get you down, do not let it control you, do not let it determine your misery or you joy."[1]

In verse 2 David states that he is crying out to the all-powerful God, "to God who fulfills his purpose for me." There's a sense in which David is saying, "I didn't choose myself to become king. God chose me. God is committed to this. I don't have to sinfully take matters into my own hands. I faithfully do my part. But God does the major part. God will accomplish all his perfect purposes for me in his perfect time in his perfect way."

In verse 3 David meditates that though God is high in the heavens he is not distant. He is an active God who draws near in power to fight for those he loves. In verse 4, as we've seen before, David honestly pours out his thoughts and feelings before the Lord. He's honest about the pain and hardship. He pulls no punches! Be honest with the Lord! He can handle your heart.

In prayer, even as we talk about ourselves to the Lord, we get our spiritual eyes off of ourselves and onto the Lord. In verse 5 David metaphorically lifts his eyes to heaven and remembers the great purpose of life. Life isn't about me nor about my hardship or my enemies. Life is ultimately about God and his glory being magnified. But he will use me and work his sovereign purposes out even through the pain and hardship of my normal life.

In verse 6 David realizes that though Saul seemed to have the upper hand, that was not actually true. God truly always has the

---

1. Lloyd-Jones, *Spiritual Depressions*, 279.

upper hand, the hand of power. God will have the last word. Saul set a trap for David. But in reality Saul would eventually fall and David would be lifted up. In Christ, we have already been lifted up and seated with him in the heavens. See Colossians 3:1–4. Remember this truth today. Hide in Christ. Hope in Christ. Be faithful. More importantly, remember his faithfulness on your part. This will bring steadfastness of heart.

## READ AND REMEMBER

Read Psalm 57 slowly.

## ASK AND ANSWER

Jot down any questions, thoughts, or insights you have here.

## WRITE AND WORSHIP

Journal through Psalm 57. Pray about your own hardships using the words of the psalm. Meditate on what it practically means to hide in God. Get your eyes off yourself and your circumstances and onto the Lord. Spend time worshipping Him. Sing the song at the end.

## O COME, LET US ADORE HIM

by John Francis Wade; translated by Frederick Oakeley

O come, let us adore Him, O come, let us adore Him, O come, let us adore Him, Christ the Lord.
We'll praise His name forever, We'll praise His name forever, We'll praise His name forever, Christ the Lord.
We'll give Him all the glory, We'll give Him all the glory, We'll give Him all the glory, Christ the Lord.
For He alone is worthy, For He alone is worthy, For He alone is worthy, Christ the Lord.

## LISTEN AND LEARN

Write any final thoughts, insights, or worshipful meditations here.

# Day 21 Psalm 59

## CHAPTER AND CONTEXT

First Samuel 19:11–18 gives us the background for the psalm. This may be the earliest psalm of David with a title. David has been faithfully serving Saul. Saul is losing his mind and becoming paranoid. He thinks David is trying to usurp his throne so he is trying to kill David. Many of us have suffered in terrible ways in life. It is comforting to know there are people in the Bible who've suffered worse.

The first four verses show David asking the Lord to deliver him. He proclaims his innocence. As we've said before, David isn't saying he's innocent before God. He is saying he is innocent before Saul. He is innocent before men for the charges that have been leveled against him. This is a good way to pray even in New Testament times. Jesus taught us to see prayer as going to a judge and asking the judge to rule in our favor when we have been wronged by an enemy. See Luke 18:1–8.

In this first section David also asks the Lord to "Awake." It may seem irreverent to ask God to wake up. The implication is that he is sleeping. It reminds me of when Jesus was literally sleeping in the boat, in the storm, with the disciples. There will be times in life when we know the right answers but we don't feel like God is near us. It does not seem to us like God is watching over us and paying attention. It seems as though he is going to let us drown.

When we face hardship like this we are often tempted to stuff our emotions. We can think it's godly to act like a stoic. It can appear spiritual to act as though we have it all together and nothing can get us down. There are many problems with this philosophy but maybe the worst is that it is a lie and it's not sustainable. It's not true. If outwardly we keep a stiff upper lip but inwardly we quake, we are telling others and probably ourselves a lie. We try to lie to God but it's totally ineffective. He knows all things. The best course of action as we've said before is to pour out our hearts before him like a raw exposed nerve. If you feel like he's asleep at the wheel of the universe, tell him. Ideally, don't do it in an arrogant accusatory way. If that's the way you address him, he's often still gracious to hear (as Jesus was in the boat) but you should later repent for this sin.

It's much better to come in honest humility. You might say, "Lord, I am being falsely accused. I hate it and it hurts and it doesn't seem fair to me. I'm trying to wait on you to rise up and fight my battles for me. But honestly it feels like you're nowhere to be found. I know this isn't true but I still wrestle with these doubts and fears. I deserve nothing from you but wrath. But you've made me great and mighty promises because of Christ's obedience in my place. Based on the blood of Christ I beg you to show me mercy and draw near. Comfort my soul but also silence my enemies!"

In verses 5 through 15 David details how evil these wicked men are. He is pleading his case with God. He's piling up the reasons God should fight for him against his attackers. David specifically asks God to punish them in verse 5 which can bother us as New Testament believers. Shouldn't we pray for our enemies? Yes, ideally we pray that God would have mercy on them first. But if they persevere in their evil and don't seem likely to repent there can come a right time and way to humbly pray that God would judge them. This should never be prayed from a place of self-righteousness that assumes we are inherently good and that there is no hope for them.

It is best to see these "imprecatory" (which essentially means to invoke a curse on someone) psalms, as many commentators call them, as a godly way to deal with your anger, fear, desire for vindication, revenge, and protection. It is a godly way to say, "I won't become a vigilante and take all my wrath out on them to defend myself. Rather I'll look away to the king on the throne of the universe and ask him to handle it for me. Maybe he will have mercy. Maybe he won't. If he chooses to have wrath on them, he will do it in a perfect time and way, which is something I can never do."

The most important thing is David is not praying these prayers in a self-centered way that is all about himself. In verse 11 David is asking God to act in such a way that "my people," meaning other believers, won't forget God, his works, and ways. In verse 13 he prays for wrath to come so that all may know that God reigns.

These are God centered prayers for God's glory and honor. These are still good model prayers for us today.

Notice how David gets his eyes off of himself and onto God, God's strength, and God's confidence in verses 8 through 10. David may tremble but God laughs. He's not scared. The psalm ends with David singing and praising God for his strength, love, and faithfulness. He feels safe. He feels heard. He feels God is near.

## READ AND REMEMBER-

Read Psalm 59 slowly.

## ASK AND ANSWER

Write down any questions or insights you may have as you read the psalm again.

## WRITE AND WORSHIP

Slowly write out this psalm in your own words. If you have any "enemies" pray for them here. Be honest with God about all the emotions of your heart, especially the negative ones. Pour out your heart before Him. Get your eyes off your weakness and onto his strength. End your time by singing the song of worship below.

# O THE DEEP, DEEP LOVE OF JESUS

by Samuel Trevor Francis

O the deep, deep love of Jesus, Vast, unmeasured, boundless free! Rolling as a mighty ocean In its fullness over me, Underneath me, all around me, Is the current of Thy love; Leading onward, leading homeward To my glorious rest above.

O the deep, deep love of Jesus, Spread His praise from shore to shore! How He loveth, ever loveth, Changeth never, nevermore; How He watches o'er His loved ones, Died to call them all His own; How for them He intercedeth, Watcheth o'er them from the throne.

O the deep, deep love of Jesus, Love of every love the best; 'Tis an ocean vast of blessing, 'Tis a haven sweet of rest, O the deep, deep love of Jesus, 'Tis a heav'n of heav'ns to me; And it lifts me up to glory, For it lifts me up to Thee.

## LISTEN AND LEARN

End by meditating on the phrase "the deep, deep love of Jesus. . . 'Tis a haven sweet of rest."

# Day 22 Psalm 63

## CHAPTER AND CONTEXT

This psalm was probably written while David fled from his son Absalom who was seeking to overthrow him as king. This must have been one of the hardest times of his life. He starts the prayer by declaring his soul's thirst for God. What exactly does this mean?

In verse 2 he mentions that there have been times in public, corporate worship where he has felt so close to God it was as though he was seeing God with his spiritual eyes. The eyes of his heart were opened to behold and worship. We should pray for a similar experience. Now that he is on the run in the wilderness he feels far from God. He doesn't feel the same close connection and he's not ok with it. He refuses to settle for the status quo.

Christians do not need to be slaves to their whims and feelings. And yet neither do we need to ignore and stuff our feelings. It is a good and godly desire to experience the presence of God. In fact Charles Spurgeon said, "it is the weightiest of all earth's sorrows for a Christian to lose the conscious presence of his covenant God."[1] David loves God. He longs for God. But he doesn't feel God. What does he do? He doesn't ignore these feelings and soldier on. He pulls aside to pray. He begs God for a fresh experience of his nearness. Is this your pattern when you feel spiritually dry?

In verse 3 David is meditating on the fact that God's saving love is better and more important than physical life itself. To live the most enjoyable human life possible but not to be in true relationship with God is truly misery. And yet, to suffer unspeakably and yet be held in the merciful and committed hand of God is to know true joy at the deepest level. Augustine says that God's love is better than the best life we can imagine.[2] This is what David is confessing and reminding himself of. He is preaching to himself.

---

1. Spurgeon, *Treasury vol. 2 part 1*, 66
2. In Spurgeon, *Treasury vol. 2 part 1*, 73.

In verse 4 David vows to praise God. Praise is a form of meditation. Take something you know to be true of God and worship him for it, even if you don't feel the reality of the truth you confess. This isn't hypocrisy if you're honest about the gap being your feelings and the facts as David is. Good meditation is forcing yourself to look at and think about God and all that is true about Him. Stay in this heart posture of prayer until your soul is stirred and you start to praise.

In verse 5 he says he believes his soul will be satisfied as with fat. He's probably again thinking of corporate worship where sacrifices were offered and a feast would follow. They often would not eat the fat portions (considered the best part, like eating a ribeye steak today that is well marbled.) But as David thinks about the joy of true worship he imagines a soul experience akin to eating the best fatty foods!

When he lays awake in bed he turns his mind to meditation. Maybe at first he couldn't sleep because of fear or worry. But he is diligent to take control of his mind and direct it to the Lord. Specifically verse 7 tells us that he remembers times when God has helped him before. He feels like a small bird hiding under its mother's wings. And when he is near unto God like that he naturally sings for joy!

Notice this level of intimacy and joy comes when one feels near unto and protected by God. The illustration he uses is of a small bird nuzzling next to its mother. Most of us don't like to think of ourselves like a small, needy, helpless bird. Our pride often makes us think we can handle things on our own, thus often preventing us from experiencing the depth of intimacy with our Father that we truly long for.

David is happy and willing to check his pride at the door and confess his deep need and utter desperation for the Lord his God to come through for him. This type of prayer and meditation leads to this type of praise, worship, and joy! Meditation makes abstract truths become experiential reality! Matthew Henry says this comes through not "transient thoughts . . . but abiding"[3] ones. Today let us pray and meditate and worship until we truly feel safe in Christ!

## READ AND REMEMBER

Read Psalm 63 once slowly.

## ASK AND ANSWER

Read it again, jotting down any thoughts, insights, or questions you have.

## WRITE AND WORSHIP-

Make Psalm 63 your own. Seek to turn each verse into a prayer, praise, or meditation of your own. Walk through the psalm verse by verse, writing out your own sentence that corresponds to each verse. At the end sing the song that follows either out loud or in your head.

3. Henry, *Henry Commentary*, 670

## JOYFUL, JOYFUL, WE ADORE THEE

by Henry van Dyke

Joyful, joyful, we adore Thee, God of glory, Lord of love; Hearts unfold like flowers before Thee, Opening to the sun above. Melt the clouds of sin and sadness, Drive the dark of doubt away; Giver of immortal gladness, Fill us with the light of day.

All Thy works with joy surround Thee, Earth and heaven reflect Thy rays, Stars and angels sing around Thee, Center of unbroken praise. Field and forest, vale and mountain, Flowery meadow, flashing sea, Chanting bird and flowing fountain, Call us to rejoice in Thee.

Thou art giving and forgiving, Ever blessing, ever blest, Wellspring of the joy of living, Ocean depth of happy rest! Thou our Father Christ, our Brother All who live in love are Thine; Teach us how to love each other, Lift us to the joy divine.

Mortals, join the happy chorus Which the morning stars began; Father love is reigning o'er us, Brother love binds man to man. Ever singing, march we onward, Victors in the midst of strife, Joyful music leads us sunward In the triumph song of life.

## LISTEN AND LEARN-

Write any thoughts here the Holy Spirit might bring to mind.

# Day 23 Psalm 90

## CHAPTER AND CONTEXT

In one sense this psalm is different than all others we've looked at. It is the only psalm attributed to Moses. It was probably written at the beginning or end of the 40 years of wondering before the nation of Israel entered the promised land. The end of the wandering seems the most likely setting for this prayer. A brief history will help.

God rescued the nation of Israel from slavery and promised to take them to a wonderful new land that would be theirs. A few months later they came to the land and sent spies in to prepare for the invasion that God promised would be successful. Two of the spies said the nation should move forward with the plan. The other 10 spies told stories of giants and fear. The nation chose not to trust God. They gave into their fears.

God disciplined them by consigning them to wander in the desert for forty years until every adult, save the two faithful spies, died. Even Moses would perish before entering the promised land because of his sin. This is an incredibly sobering story.

We don't know exactly, but likely somewhere between one to three million people left Egypt and began the journey. So many of those people were sentenced to die over a forty year period. And Moses was appointed to lead and guide them as they walked in circles and slowly waited to die. It's somewhat depressing.

Have you ever felt consigned to suffer? Have you ever been filled with despair? Have you ever thought your life was purposeless? Surely Moses and the perishing Israelites must have felt that way.

As Moses thinks of all those deaths he penned this psalm. He starts by comparing the frailty of humanity with the eternity of God the creator. Acts 17:28 teaches that we all live in God. Yet we are surrounded with death, despair, and decay. It may be that Moses is meditating on Genesis 1–3 (which he also wrote) as he writes this psalm.

God is eternal, good, and strong. We are temporal, sinful, and weak. We are frail, fragile, and fickle. Even the best of us sins, gets sick, and dies.

Our suffering, hardship, sickness, and death are not ultimately generic or random. You can trace them all back to Genesis 3. All pain and sadness in this life find their root in Adam's rebellion. We all live under a curse in this world. God is angry at sin. We deserve the pain we get. We actually all deserve the full wrath and fury of God. Yet God in His great love and mercy lets all people experience much of his goodness on this planet! See Matthew 5:45.

Verse 11 is interesting. Who can really, fully understand the depth of God's anger and wrath in a fully appropriate way? No mere man. Even those who suffer in hell eternally will not fully know his wrath for it is never ending. Only one man properly considers God's power, anger, and wrath; the Lord Jesus Christ. He stared into the full cup of God's wrath in Gethsemane. He begged mercy. His request was denied. He went to the cross and hung in shame under the full weight of God's righteous fury at sin. He bore the anger that all his people earned.

What should be our response to such glorious and sobering truths? We must take God and our lives seriously. We must learn to live circumspectly all our days. We must beg God for mercy even as we face death, despair, and hardship in this life.

We must look past this life to experience true joy. We must awake each day looking to him to fill our souls and not to even the best things this world has to offer. He can and will give true happiness even in the worst of circumstances we face. For all those in Christ, the only truly damning circumstances have already been suffered for us! Plead with God today for joy. Beg for more joy than pain. Pray for gladness to eclipse suffering!

The Israelites consigned to die in the wilderness could've understandably felt a gigantic sense of purposelessness. Yet Moses is wise to end this psalm praying for the next generation. All the parents would die in the desert. The children would go and inherit the land. He begs that they would see and know God afresh in power and glory.

His prayer was answered. Read the book of Joshua. It is primarily the story of faithful and godly people conquering the land for God's glory and their joy. Beg God today for favor and that his blessing and smile would rest on your life and work to "establish the work of our hands!" Pray that he will bless the next generation of believers as well.

## READ AND REMEMBER

Read Psalm 90 slowly and soberly.

## ASK AND ANSWER

Write down any thoughts or questions here as you read it again.

## WRITE AND WORSHIP

Slowly journal through Psalm 90. Write a sentence in your own words from each verse. Compare your present life with God's eternal life. Compare your hardship with his joy; your weakness with his strength. Spend time meditating on the song at the end.

## O GOD, OUR HELP IN AGES PAST

by Isaac Watts

O God, our help in ages past, Our hope for years to come, Our shelter from the stormy blast, And our eternal home!

Under the shadow of Thy Throne Thy saints have dwelt secure; Sufficient is Thine arm alone, And our defense is sure.

Before the hills in order stood, Or earth received her frame, From everlasting Thou art God, To endless years the same.

A thousand ages in Thy sight Are like an evening gone; Short as the watch that ends the night, Before the rising sun.

Time, like an ever rolling stream, Bears all its sons away; They fly, forgotten, as a dream Dies at the op'ning day.

O God, our help in ages past, Our hope for years to come, Be Thou our guide while life shall last, And our eternal home. Amen.

## LISTEN AND LEARN

Write any last thoughts or worshipful insights here.

# Day 24 Psalm 103

## CHAPTER AND CONTEXT

This psalm starts with meditation. David is preaching to himself. He is speaking to his own soul. He is commanding his whole being to praise God. Bless is the opposite of curse. It's doing all you can to help or praise someone else.

Meditation is the opposite of spiritual forgetfulness. It is an intentional remembering, a purposeful retelling to yourself. When I was young and forgot to do a chore at home I thought that was a valid excuse. I would say, "Sorry I forgot to take the trash out this morning. I just didn't think of it. I didn't mean to forget, it was an accident." My dad would respond: "Mean not to." For years I didn't understand what he meant, but it slowly dawned on me. He meant don't be mentally lazy. Don't be haphazard with my responsibilities. Be intentional about remembering. I should have purposefully written myself a note and stuck it on the bathroom mirror if that is what it took so that I wouldn't forget. I didn't like that saying. But now I use it with my own kids!

We can debate whether that's a good parental example. But it is certainly excellent spiritual advice. When my kids were younger they often found something to complain about. One might say, "My life stinks because I don't have the brand new iPhone like all my friends! Life is so unfair! I think I deserve a new phone now dad! Why can't I have it?!"

I'd often respond by telling them to get a piece of paper and write down thirty good things about their lives. They'd say, "I can't think of 30 good things." I'd say, "Start with basic things like clean air to breathe and running water to drink."

What was I trying to do? I was attempting to help them get their eyes off of the one or two hardships in their lives and onto the countless good things God had already given. I wanted them to have happy and humble hearts.

That's essentially what David does in this psalm. If you are in Christ, God has legally forgiven all your sin, past, present, and future. That's enough to sing hallelujah over! But he goes further. He heals us. If he doesn't heal you in this life, He will in the next and it's coming real soon. He blesses and satisfies your life with his love and many other good things! Rejoice!

Derek Kidner says David is "rousing . . . himself to shake off apathy or gloom . . . [and] using his mind and memory to kindle emotions."[1] Tim Keller agrees, "We are not helpless before our emotions. Meditation is a very assertive way of bringing the truth to our hearts and emotions, sometimes almost pummeling them into submission."[2] Charles Spurgeon teaches that we shouldn't give God half-hearted praise: "We have need, again and again to bestir ourselves when we are about to worship God, for it would be shameful to offer him anything less than the utmost . . . [Our heart] needs spurring to its duty . . . God's all cannot be praised with less than our all."[3]

Keller further comments on the second part of verse 4: "God imparts an experience of his love to us in a way that makes us feel honored and built up."[4] Some of us rarely experience this. Some of us may not even believe it is possible. But that is the reason we must be aggressive, disciplined, faithful, and focused in our meditation. We must work, with His empowering grace, to bring our wandering hearts and minds into line with spiritual reality. We must taste and see that the Lord is good (Psalm 34:8).

In verses 6 and 7 the Old Testament story of salvation is recounted and remembered and celebrated. Starting in verse 8 the meditation focuses on God as our loving Father. He may discipline us. But it's always for our good. He loves us so much. He loves us better than the best human father could!

1. Kidner, *Psalms* 73–150, 397.
2. Keller, *Praying with the Psalms*, 40–41.
3. Spurgeon, *Treasury vol. 2 part 2*, 275–6.
4. Keller, *Praying with the Psalms*, 42.

Matthew Henry says, "He's never been rigorous and severe with us."[5] If He wasn't a God of patience, we would have all been in hell long ago. God has tender compassion for us. He knows and understands our weaknesses and frailty. He has eternally separated us from the punishment our sins deserve. Christ has paid the price in full. We are free forever. Let us sing, rejoice, meditate, and wonder!

## READ AND REMEMBER

Read the whole psalm slowly.

## ASK AND ANSWER

Read it again jotting down thoughts and questions here.

## WRITE AND WORSHIP

Journal through the whole psalm slowly. Intentionally call to mind specific ways God has personally blessed you. Turn those thoughts into prayer and worship. End by singing the song at the end.

5. Henry, *Henry Commentary*, 716.

# HOLY, HOLY, HOLY

by Reginald Heber

Holy, Holy, Holy! Lord God Almighty! Early in the morning our song shall rise to Thee; Holy, holy, holy! Merciful and mighty! God in three Persons, blessed Trinity!

Holy, holy, holy! all the saints adore Thee, Casting down their golden crowns around the glassy sea; Cherubim and seraphim falling down before Thee, Which wert and art and evermore shalt be.

Holy, holy, holy! though the darkness hide Thee, Though the eye of sinful man Thy glory may not see; Only Thou art holy there is none beside Thee, Perfect in pow'r in love and purity.

Holy, holy, holy! Lord God Almighty! All Thy works shall praise Thy name in earth and sky and sea; Holy, holy, holy! Merciful and mighty! God in three Persons, blessed Trinity!

## LISTEN AND LEARN

Write down any last thoughts the Holy Spirit might bring to mind.

# Day 25 Psalm 119

## CHAPTER AND CONTEXT

Psalm 119 is the longest chapter in the whole Bible. You probably won't be able to meditate on the whole thing in one day and maybe you shouldn't even try. Someone said that Psalm 119 is a love song for God's word. This is a great picture of someone meditating on the word of God in a very direct way.

At least two things come out clearly in the first eight verses. One is the similarity with Psalm 1. Those who are truly happy are those who meditate on and obey God's word. Not only will they be happy in this life, but also in the next. They will never ultimately be ashamed.

Secondly we see a theme that will prevail throughout all 176 verses. There are pledges to do my part to be serious about walking in obedience: "I will keep your statues;" (Psalm 119:8a) side by side and interlaced with prayers for God's help, "do not utterly forsake me!" (Psalm 119:8b). Here is my plan to obey right beside my plea for help to obey!

Many different words and phrases are used throughout this psalm to describe God's word: the law of the Lord, testimonies, precepts, statues, commandments, rules. They all have slightly different nuances but refer to the same thing: God's holy, infallible, and trustworthy words to his people. The psalmist loves and longs for God and his word. He pledges himself to trust and obey God's word. He is committed to suffer for the word if need be. Virtually every verse mentions the word of God in some form or fashion.

Verses 9–11 begin to make this psalm very practical. All people struggle with sinful temptations but at times young men seem to struggle with them the most. How can humans in the hardest seasons of life fight against sin but by memorizing and meditating on God's word? We take it into our most inner being until it becomes part of who we are. John MacArthur says,

"Internalizing the word is a believer's best weapon to defend against encroaching sin."[1]

Verse 12 shows the psalmist breaking into worship. Meditation, prayer, and worship should seamlessly flow together as we have tried to demonstrate throughout this book. In verse 13 he states that he doesn't keep the word to himself but shares it with others. In verse 14 he remembers how the word of God brings more joy than money can ever buy.

In verse 16 he pledges to continue delighting in God's word by intentionally remembering it as we discussed yesterday. In verse 17 he prays for God's blessings. But notice what kind of blessings he specifically asks for. He doesn't ask for more money, fame, or a nicer house (although those prayers aren't always necessarily wrong.) No, he prays that God would bless him in such a way to make him faithful. He's asking for power to keep him holy, motivated, and disciplined in walking according to God's plan. He's praying for sanctification. Is that truly one of the burning desires of your heart? Does it fill your prayer requests at times? It should!

I once heard John Piper say that he prays verse 18 most mornings before he reads his Bible. He asks God to illuminate his eyes. Pray today (and every day) that God would make words jump off the page to you. Ask the Lord to personalize and apply his word to your everyday life as you read. Beg him to open the eyes of your heart to have more insight than you ever have before. Plead with him to mercifully instruct you in deeper truths that you may not have been ready for before. Persevere in these prayers with an honest heart and he will eventually answer. Don't give up!

In verses 19–24 he meditates on the fact that he is a stranger on planet earth. The earth is filled with and ruled by evil people. A saint is out of place on planet earth. We deeply and desperately need God's word to satisfy and sustain us.

There will be times when it feels like the whole world is against us. There may be times when we are literally persecuted by the rulers of this dark kingdom. But even if Satan himself opposes us, God's word gives us all we need for life and godliness. It is able

---

1. MacArthur, *The MacArthur Study Bible*, 851.

to fully equip us for all good works (2 Timothy 3:12–17). All the counsel for life we need is here. Go deep in meditation today.

## READ AND REMEMBER

Read the first 50 verses of the psalm slowly.

## ASK AND ANSWER

Read the first 24 verses of the psalm again noting any questions you have.

## WRITE AND WORSHIP

Journal through the first 24 verses of this psalm. Focus on the pattern of pledging to obey while also pleading for help to pray. Let the Lord lead you into fresh awe and wonder.

## HOW FIRM A FOUNDATION

by John Rippon

How firm a foundation, ye saints of the Lord, Is laid for your faith in His excellent Word! What more can He say than to you He hath said, To you who for refuge to Jesus have fled?

"Fear not, I am with Thee; O be not dismayed, For I am thy God, and will still give thee aid; I'll strengthen thee, help thee, and cause thee to stand, Upheld by My righteous, omnipotent hand.

"When through fiery trials thy pathway shall lie, My grace, all sufficient, shall be thy supply: The flame shall not hurt thee; I only design Thy dross to consume and thy gold to refine.

"The soul that on Jesus hath leaned for repose I will not, I will not desert to its foes; That soul, though all hell should endeavor to shake, I'll never, no, never, no never forsake!"

## LISTEN AND LEARN

Spend extra time meditating on the last two verses. Then write down any final insights here.

# Day 26 Psalm 127

## CHAPTER AND CONTEXT

There are two psalms that claim Solomon as the author in the title. This is one. I call this psalm the workaholic's warning. If you read what Kings and Chronicles have to say about Solomon you'll see he accomplished very much in his day. This psalm is a meditation and instruction on how to work the right way, specifically, how to work as unto the Lord (Colossians 3:23).

Solomon starts with the assumption that there is a type of work that stands the test of time and one that doesn't. No one really wants to work hard at something only to have it crumble soon after. This psalm can be applied to virtually any task, whether that's building a house, a city, a church, or a family. It could also be applied to leading and growing a business, a marriage, or even a whole country. The point is we all have an innate God-implanted desire for our work to count, to matter, to last.

If we seek to work in an independent way, our works will eventually fail. They will be in vain. The word vain means worthless or empty. The solution isn't that we quit working or give up. Notice Solomon doesn't tell the construction worker to lay down his hammer and just sleep all day. He doesn't advise the city watchman to leave his post. Rather, he encourages us in whatever we do to do our best but do it in a spirit of dependence.

If God doesn't work with us, in us, and through us then all our best attempts will be futile. If God doesn't bless the work of our hands as Moses prayed in Psalm 90, our works won't outlast us in any type of permanent or good way. The real secret to this is praying and entrusting all things to Christ. Christ told us we could do nothing of significance without him. But He also said that with him living in and through us, the fruit of our lives would remain (John 15:5, 16).

On the outside, to the mere human eye, an independent worker and a dependent worker might look exactly the same. They might get up at the same hour, arrive at work with a similar facial expressions, and sweat the same amount as the day goes on. So how can we know for ourselves if we are working in a true spirit of dependence or independence?

One way is to ask yourself if you are doing restful work or restless work. One clear sign is that if you are constantly burning the candle at both ends, you are probably not trusting the Lord enough. It's not sin to wake up early. It seems Jesus usually did. It's not sin to stay up late sometimes. We know of at least one night Jesus stayed up all night. But if the consistent pattern of your life is to neglect the sleep your body and mind needs, that is a bad sign. That might be necessary in a certain season of crisis or combat. It should not be the norm.

God likes sleep. He invented it as a great gift for his kids. Even the Lord Jesus took naps at times! I heard a pastor say once, "Sometimes the most spiritual thing you can do is take a nap!" God gives us sleep as a gift but he also gives to us while we sleep. He doesn't rest or slumber (Psalm 121:4). He doesn't get tired or weary (Isaiah 40:29–31). He keeps running the universe just fine without you while you spend one fourth to one third of your whole life unconscious!

He's God and we aren't! Don't eat "the bread of anxious toil" (Psalm 127:2b). Worry is a sin at all times and in all places (Philippians 4:6–7). Worry is a sign that you are trying to be God, to play God, to bear the weight on your soul that only he can. Worry is a practical way you say to God "I think I could do a better job of running my corner of the universe than you are right now!" It's a terrible way to live. Not only is it sinful. It's stupid. It won't work. And it crushes your soul in the process.

Wake up each day and do your best with what's before you. But ask for the Lord's help before you begin and as you go then at the end of your day, give it all back to him in prayer. Roll your burdens onto the Lord. Let him handle them while you sleep. He will act. He will accomplish all his purposes for you!

The sin under the sin in all this is that most of us really want control. It is not enough for us to be faithful with our assigned duties. Rather we want to demand of the Lord certain results. That's where our worry comes from. We must obey and trust him with the results and the timing of the results, which is often the main issue.

This psalm ends speaking of children which, for many people, is where most of our worries lie. Even in having children, there's a role mom and dad have to play to make a baby. But it's ultimately all up to the Lord when and how and if he blesses our works to make them fruitful. That's true of all life. Do your part. Enjoy the process. Trust the Lord's timing and purposes.

## READ AND REMEMBER

Read Psalm 127 slowly.

## ASK AND ANSWER

Read it again and write down any thoughts or questions you have.

## WRITE AND WORSHIP

Journal through Psalm 127. Turn each line into a personal prayer, confession, praise, or meditation. Sing the hymn at the end.

## COME, THOU FOUNT OF EVERY BLESSING

by Robert Robinson; adapted by Margaret Clarkson

Come, Thou Fount of every blessing, Tune my heart to sing Thy grace; Streams of mercy, never ceasing, Call for songs of loudest praise. Teach me some melodious sonnet, Sung by flaming tongues above; Praise His name I'm fixed upon it Name of God's redeeming love.
Hitherto Thy love has blest me; Thou hast bro't me to this place; And I know Thy hand will bring me Safely home by Thy good grace. Jesus sought me when a stranger, Wandering from the fold of God; He, to rescue me from danger, Brought me with His precious blood. O to grace how great a debtor Daily I'm constrained to be! Let Thy goodness, like a fetter, Bind my wandering heart to Thee: Prone to wander, Lord, I feel it, Prone to leave the God I love; Here's my heart, O take and seal it; Seal it for Thy courts above. Amen.

## LISTEN AND LEARN

Write down any thoughts the Holy Spirit might bring to mind or impress on your heart.

# Day 27 Psalm 131

## CHAPTER AND CONTEXT

We don't know for sure when this was written though most commentators I've read agree that it was when Saul persecuted David. At minimum the lessons David learned and wrestled with during those days are evident in this psalm. These lessons are very applicable to our lives.

Saul and Saul's men accused David of arrogance. They accused him of setting his ambitions too high. They accused him of trying to usurp Saul's throne. David knows he has no real recourse with Saul and his henchmen so he appeals to a higher power, the King of all kings.

David starts his prayer pleading his humility. This almost sounds arrogant to tell God how humble you are. But David is essentially saying, "Lord you know what they say about me isn't true. I've not acted towards them in pride. I've tried by your grace to live humbly." But it actually goes further than that.

In the second half of verse 1 David means, "I don't involve myself with things too difficult for me." In modern day language he might say, "I don't concern myself with things above my pay grade." Think about this for a moment. He has been appointed to be king of all God's people. In some ways he functioned like a prophet because he was also being used by God to write Scripture. He might be the greatest man living on planet earth in his day. Yet he's humble and self-aware enough to know that there is a whole other plane of influence and power that is far above him. This is true of all of us whether we like it or not, whether we care to admit it or not.

David was anointed to be king as a teenager and then had to wait for over a decade, maybe as many as fourteen years, to actually become king. Much of that time was not spent in the palace as a loyal number two to an aging king. Nor did he get the glory of being a great general all those days. Most of those days he lived as a felon and a fugitive on the run, a beggar and a vagabond.

Imagine the tension of the promise made over his life versus the day to day reality of his life. He must have often wrestled with three questions. Why is this happening to me? When will it be over? How will it end? See 1 Samuel 26:10 for one example of his thought process.

It's not wrong to ask questions like these. We probably all struggle with them at times. But there is a humble, godly way to wrestle and there is a proud, sinful way. This prayer can help us steer clear of this sin.

Sin creeps in when we demand an answer and act as though we have a right to know. This may have been part of Adam and Eve's original sin in Genesis 3:5–6. "If there is some special knowledge that God and the serpent have, why can't we have it? We want it! That's not fair. That's not right! We have a right to know! Why can't we eat of this one tree?! We want to have the forbidden fruit right now!" It didn't end well for them and neither will such an attitude help us out.

The second way that such questions can become sin is if in the absence of answers, we refuse to be content. If we can't stand to wait on God's ways and timing, we often take matters into our own hands, even if it means breaking a few rules to get there. Whether that means eating forbidden fruit, killing a crazy king, or something in between, there is never an excuse to break God's word.

There is a secret to contentment in this life that can be learned but it doesn't come easy. Paul spoke of it in Philippians 4:11. David speaks of it in verse 2. Have you ever seen a nursing child with its mother when it is hungry but not being fed yet? It is angry, demanding, and impatient. It often screams. Its little head will bob around looking for milk.

Practically speaking the baby thinks of the mom as a milk wagon. She serves a utilitarian function. To some degree the baby uses the mom for what mom can give the baby. We often treat God the same way. We use him. We demand from him. We are easily angered when things don't go exactly our way. We act as though he owes us good things.

A weaned child has learned to trust. A weaned child has learned to wait. A weaned child has months if not years of mom faithfully showing up and providing even if it isn't as quickly as the baby would like. A weaned child can be with mom in a contented spirit and just enjoy mom for mom's sake without demanding food. We should have such a relationship with our heavenly Father.

Some of you may say, "But God hasn't proved himself to me. I've not experienced enough of his faithfulness to fully trust him." Look to the cross. The God-man Jesus wrestled with the same questions David did in the garden of Gethsemane and on the cross. God never answered him in the way Jesus wanted. He let Jesus suffer hell for the sins of others. If we trust in his finished work for us, we can come to the Father relationally, like a weaned, happy, content, humble child. God will provide what's best for us, in the best way at the best time.

## READ AND REMEMBER

Read Psalm 131 slowly.

## ASK AND ANSWER

Read it again and write down any thoughts or questions here.

## WRITE AND WORSHIP

Write out Psalm 131 slowly in your own words. Take your time. Go deep. Really seek to express all your feelings, doubts, fears, and concerns to him. Do all you can to meet with God and worship him today experientially. Sing the hymn at the end.

## JUST A CLOSER WALK WITH THEE

by Fanny J. Crosby

I am weak but Thou art strong; Jesus, keep me from all wrong; I'll be satisfied as long As I walk, let me walk close to Thee.

Thro' this world of toils and snares, If I falter, Lord, who cares? Who with me my burden shares? None but Thee, dear Lord, none but Thee.

When my feeble life is o'er, Time for me will be no more; Guide me gently, safely o'er To Thy kingdom shore, to Thy shore.

Just a closer walk with Thee, Grant it, Jesus, is my plea, Daily, walking close to Thee, Let it be, dear Lord, let it be.

## LISTEN AND LEARN

Write any final insights here.

# Day 28 Psalm 138

This Psalm was likely written between 2 Samuel 5 and 7. In David's early days as king he was very successful. He went from strength to strength. Many of us pray regularly "when all around our soul gives way."[1] But how do we pray when all our days seem blessed and abounding with God's goodness? Sometimes it takes more discipline and focus to faithfully seek God on days when the sun shines brightest.

There is a temptation when all goes well to let the victories go to our heads. There are multiple ways to do this. One is outright pride that arrogantly takes credit for all that is good and right in our lives: "I did this!" The other is a form of presumption that blandly acknowledges that God gave the victory but doesn't really worship him sincerely for the blessing. It is an attitude that just assumes that God is supposed to bless me. It is also a type of self-centered, self-righteous, deserving mentality. Lastly we can merely be passive and not slow down and smell the roses. We must learn to intentionally pause, notice all the good that has been given to us, and then let that gratitude turn into true worship and praise that flows to God from the deepest parts of our being. We see David doing that in this psalm.

He starts by looking back in the first three verses. David has had much military success. In 2 Samuel 5 David routs the Philistines, the arch enemies of God's people. They flee and leave their "gods" (idols) behind. David's men burn them. David sees his earthly victory as a spiritual victory of Yahweh over the pagan gods and whatever demons may be behind them. This is intentional, sincere praise. He is not merely going through the motions. He is truly worshipping. He is prioritizing taking time to give God credit. Do you regularly slow down and do this?

Christians should learn to treat glory, praise, and credit like a hot potato. When it is given to you, get rid of it quickly. Give it back to God. When all seems to go right for you and many others praise you and celebrate your gifts and wisdom, go get alone.

1. Mote, "The Solid Rock," 402.

Maybe even lay on your face prostrate and tangibly turn your hands up to heaven and tell the Lord that he is the true and only victor. Any success you have is from, for, and by him. This will keep you in the safe place of a humble heart.

The last part of verse 2 is hard to translate. But the essential meaning is: "Your word is your bond. When you give your word, you always keep it, even if it hurts. Your promises to me are as real and trustworthy as you are in yourself." God had promised to make David king. He had done it. We can trust him. When our prayers are answered, pause to give him praise.

David had prayed to be faithful and courageous as he ran from Saul and as he led Israel's armies into battle. God had answered him and given him all the internal stamina he needed. God will do the same for you. Alec Mortyer, an expert in Hebrew, says God invigorated his soul.[2] Often we know what we ought to do but seem to have no willpower to be faithful. Ask God to give you all the internal motivation you need to fully obey, in all times, places, and ways.

In verses 4 and 5 David meditates on the future praise that will come to God. He says one day all kings of the earth will praise the Lord. This never happened in David's day and still hasn't. It is a prediction of the end of time when every knee will bow and every tongue confess that the one true Son of David is the King of kings and Lord of lords (Philippians 2:9–11). The fact that that day is coming should fill all God's people with great joy, gratitude, hope, and confidence, no matter what we face today or tomorrow. Adoniram Judson, the missionary, famously said, "the future is as bright as the promises of God."

Verse 6 expresses a great truth that should lead us all to worship. God is high and holy. He rightly ought to destroy us all in our sin for our arrogant rebellion. But when, by his grace, we humble ourselves before him in honesty about our weakness, sin, and neediness, he is drawn to us. He takes notice of us. He loves us, comes near to us, saves us, secures us, sanctifies us, and will one day glorify us!

---

2. Motyer, *Psalms by the Day*, 396.

David ends this psalm by proclaiming his confidence that God will once again deliver and bless him. Past performance is the best predictor of future performance. God's record is perfect. "There is no shadow of turning with" him.[3] He can be trusted.

In verse 8 David sums up the whole psalm. God will accomplish all his good purposes for me (Romans 8:28). He praises him for his steadfast, faithful, covenant love. Then he ends praying that God would be faithful and stay true to his character. Praying that God would act is one of the surest signs we believe his promises that he will.

## READ AND REMEMBER

Read the psalm slowly.

## ASK AND ANSWER

Read it again, jotting down any thoughts or questions here.

## WRITE AND WORSHIP

Slowly journal through the psalm in your own words. Turn each phrase into either a meditation on God's character, a moment of worship, or a prayer for God to act. End by worshipping through the hymn at the end.

3. Chisholm, "Great is Thy Faithfulness," 43.

# TAKE MY LIFE AND LET IT BE

by Frances Ridley Havergal

Take my life and let it be Consecrated, Lord, to Thee, Take my moments and my days Let them flow in ceaseless praise, Let them flow in ceaseless praise.

Take my hands and let them move At the impulse of Thy love; Take my feet and let them be Swift and beautiful for Thee, Swift and beautiful for Thee.

Take my voice and let me sing Always, only, for my King; Take my lips and let them be Filled with messages from Thee, Filled with messages from Thee.

Take my silver and my gold Not a mite would I withhold; Take my intellect and use Ev'ry pow'r as Thou shalt choose, Ev'ry pow'r as Thou shalt choose.

Take my will and make it Thine It shall be no longer mine; Take my heart it is Thine own, It shall be Thy royal throne, It shall be Thy royal throne.

## LISTEN AND LEARN

Write any final thoughts or insights here.

# Day 29 Psalm 143

## CHAPTER AND CONTEXT

This psalm was likely written when David was running from Absalom, his son, who was trying to overthrow him. So many of David's Psalms were written during hardship. When we are suffering we should remember that God often meets us the most when we are hurting and low.

From the beginning David grounds the whole prayer on God's faithful character and not in his own merit. He knows he has no right to God based on his own life record. Our sins have cut us all off from God's goodness. If God didn't initiate to us in covenant love to save us there would be no hope.

Imagine a man who invested all his money in a business venture. His father strongly counseled him not to do it. He did it anyway and lost all his money. If he came back to his father to ask for some help to get back on his feet, he couldn't plead his wisdom or his faithfulness as a good son. His actions have ruined both of those arguments. All he could really argue is that his father was a good father who loved his kids even when they didn't deserve it. That's how David prays. That's how we should pray. We have no merit in ourselves. We only have the merit of Christ imputed to us by faith. But that is more than enough.

David is desperate and suffering and that's why he runs to God so earnestly in prayer. It seems he is depressed and filled with despair. He has nowhere else to turn. God is his only hope and he knows this. He feels the reality of this fact. He is utterly and completely dependent on God. This is always the case, but we often forget it in times of strength. When the world falls apart around us, it often serves as a stark reminder that we have no true hope outside of the Lord.

What does David do in the worst of times? He meditates and muses. He remembers God's deeds and character. He calls to mind God's past ways with him and all his deliverances. He preaches truth to himself. He reminds himself of his past history and experience with God.

"Meditation is prayer's handmaid . . . before and after the performance of supplication. It is as the plough before the sower, to prepare the heart for the duty of prayer."[1] As we mature in faith we should naturally learn to intermingle our prayers and our meditations. Often it will be the case that we cannot easily and clearly delineate where one stops and the other starts. Our prayers and meditations should flow in and out of one another.

In verse 8 David asks to hear of God's steadfast love in the morning. This again implies the urgency that David feels. It is not enough to merely intellectually know of God's love. He needs to feel and experience it first thing in the morning so that he is not plunged into despair as he surveys his circumstances.

John Gil says that he is asking for a "more distinct knowledge" of God's word.[2] He is asking for illumination. He is asking for God to draw near in a special and fresh way and open the eyes of his heart to behold wonderful things from God's law he had never noticed before (Psalm 119:18).

Notice that David does not plan to be passive in whatever deliverance God may devise. His attitude isn't a lazy presumption that God will fight for him if he perseveres in hard hearted ignoring of God. Rather, he pledges to obey. He wants to obey. He asks for grace and wisdom to know where and how to obey. He knows that God must and will do the major part in protecting him. Yet he acknowledges in verse 8 and 10 that he has a part to play and that he will gladly play it.

He is asking for more than mere wisdom on what to do. He is asking that God would help and enable him to follow through and persevere in obedience. Derek Kidner says David is asking for "an inward work of inclining the heart and awakening the mind."[3] There will be seasons where we know what to do but don't want to

---

1. Gurnall quoted in Spurgeon, *Treasury vol. 3 part 2*, 343.

2. Gil, *Psalms*, 300.

3. Kidner, *Psalms 73–150*, 513.

obey. It is good, right, and wise to pray that God would change the desires of our heart to bring them in line with His.

The prayer in the last verse for God to "cut off my enemies" may still bother us. But Mortyer is helpful here. "[T]he mere need of his people is powerful before God. . .There are circumstances (like David's) where there is no deliverance without destruction and to pray for the one is to pray for the other."[4] God saved his people ultimately at the cross. But the cross was also the death blow to our greatest enemy, Satan and all his minions. Pray in confidence today.

## READ AND REMEMBER

Read Psalm 143 slowly.

## ASK AND ANSWER

Write down any thoughts, insights, or questions here.

## WRITE AND WORSHIP

Write your own prayer and meditation expressing your desperation and dependence on God here. End by singing the hymn that follows.

---

4. Mortyer, "Psalms," 580.

# PASS ME NOT

by Fanny J. Crosby

Pas me not, O gentle Savior Hear my humble cry! While on others Thou art calling, Do not pass me by.

Let me at a throne of mercy Find a sweet relief; Kneeling there in deep contrition- Help my unbelief.

Trusting only in Thy merit, Would I seek Thy face; Heal my wounded, broken spirit, Save me by Thy grace.

Thou the spring of all my comfort, More than life to me! Whom have I on earth beside Thee? Whom in heav'n but Thee?

Savior, Savior, Hear my humble cry! While on others Thou art calling, Do not pass me by.

## LISTEN AND LEARN

Write any final thoughts or insights here.

# Day 30 Psalm 145

## CHAPTER AND CONTEXT

This is the last psalm ascribed to David. It is filled with praise. We don't know when it was written but it works in any life setting. It is a broken acrostic, meaning that each line starts with the next letter of the Hebrew alphabet, with one letter *n* (nun) left out. This is probably done intentionally to say that although we can know God truly, we will never know him exhaustively.

God is infinite. The display of his goodness and glory is without end. His majesty is incomprehensible. But that shouldn't stop us from trying.

Even in heaven we will never stop learning of the infinite ocean of God's greatness. Eternity will not be boring. We will spend forever seeing, learning, and worshipping some new facet of the beauty of our God and Savior. David seems to be reveling in this reality in this psalm.

The theme of the psalm seems to be that God is worthy of worship. God is so great that we are compelled to praise Him. If we honestly look at his creation and take note of his character we cannot help but break out in wonder and delight. Christians should enjoy worshipping God and should do it every day. When we don't feel like worshipping we shouldn't "fake it until we make it." Rather, we should repent of our dullness and ask God to open the eyes of our heart to behold his glory all around us and appreciate it as deeply as we should.

True worship is rarely content to keep to itself. When we are overflowing with praising and delighting in the Lord there is an impulse to draw others in. Notice how David does this in verse 4.

The first seven verses seem to focus on God's attributes in relation to creation. Looking at creation should lead to worship. But in verse 8 there is a shift. David begins to marvel at the splendor of God's grace in relationship to his creatures, specifically humans who have rebelled. God is a tender Father, slow to anger, and quick to show mercy.

Our God is friendly. He has pity and compassion on strugglers. He knows that we are overwhelmed with our sin debt and he doesn't disdain us for that. If we come to him humbly, he will meet us with mercy!

The ESV Study Bible, commenting on verse 8 says, "Showing wrath isn't God's preferred option."[1] God loves to show mercy. He delights in it. He is just and the justifier of the one who has faith in Jesus (Romans 3:26). This is truly the pinnacle of his glory and we should easily get lost in wonder as we magnify him for his mercy and saving grace.

The New American Standard Bible translates Isaiah 53:10 to say, "the Lord was pleased to crush Him." God so loved the world that he was willing to exhaust his wrath on Jesus for his people! It almost seems to be blasphemous to say it but it's true! I was sharing the gospel with a friend one day. He interrupted me and said, "But it's too good to be true!?" I said, "I know! But it is true!"

Verse 9 is not teaching universalism. It's teaching the same truth Matthew 5:45 does: God even gives the worst sinners some grace in that they get to enjoy so many of his good gifts in this life on this planet before they perish! Verse 10 shows us that even evil and inanimate objects praise God to some degree as they reflect back to God the fact that he is their creator. Matthew Henry says, "All God's works do praise him, as the beautiful building praises the builder or the well-drawn picture praises the painter."[2]

The last seven verses of the psalm reiterate the fact that God loves to give good gifts to his children. He delights in his own generosity. He is not stingy. He is not a bare minimum God. He loves to pour out his grace, mercy, goodness, and kindness richly. He is lavish in all his ways!

He doesn't give any of us exactly what we want, when we want, and how we want it all the time. But if we knew all that he knows we would clearly see that he is always giving us precisely what is

1. Collins, "Psalms," 1123.

2. Henry, *Henry Commentary*, 757.

best for us in the long run according to his perfect plan. David ends with a longing for all people to bless his holy name. This should be our prayer and hope as well. And Philippians 2:9–11 promises us that it will one day be true! God will get all the praise and glory he deserves!

## READ AND REMEMBER

Read the psalm through once in its entirety.

## ASK AND ANSWER

Read it again, more slowly this time. Write down any thoughts, insights, or questions you have.

## WRITE AND WORSHIP

Write this psalm out in your own words. Mainly focus on praising, worshiping, and thanking God. As requests come up, intersperse them with your other meditations. But mainly focus on praise today. Sing the hymn at the end.

## MY JESUS, I LOVE THEE

by William R. Featherston

My Jesus, I love Thee, I know Thou art mine For Thee all the follies of sin I resign; My gracious Redeemer, my Savior art Thou: If ever I loved Thee, my Jesus, 'tis now.

I love Thee because Thou hast first loved me And purchased my pardon on Calvary's tree; I love Thee for wearing the thorns on Thy brow: If ever I loved Thee, my Jesus, 'tis now.

I'll love Thee in life, I will love Thee in death, And praise Thee as long as Thou lendest me breath; And say when the death-dew lies cold on my brow, "If ever I loved Thee, my Jesus, 'tis now."

In mansions of glory and endless delight, I'll ever adore Thee in heaven so bright; I'll sing with the glittering crown on my brow, "If ever I loved I loved Thee, my Jesus, 'tis now."

## LISTEN AND LEARN

Write any final worshipful thoughts here.

# Day 31 Psalm 148

## CHAPTER AND CONTEXT

As the book of Psalms nears an end the psalms seem more filled with praise. Many of the psalms we have looked at are filled with pain, sorrow, despair, and gloom. Often praise and hope break through by the end of the psalm. But this psalm does not fit this pattern. Psalm 148 starts and ends overflowing with praise. It calls for all created things, living and inanimate, to give praise to their Creator. We should obey this psalm!

Verses 11 and 12 call on all people to praise God. You don't have to be a worship leader or pastor to be swept up in the praise of your God! Verse 13 reminds us that in the end, all praise, glory, and honor will go to God and God alone. This psalm seems to usher us into the end of all things and the beginning of the new heavens and earth that will be perfectly filled and consumed with pure praise. This psalm is a coronation of sorts of the consummation of God's perfect plan on earth being finished and celebrated. We should look forward to that day and hour with great hope. We should learn to meditate on heaven and the glories that await us there.

I want us mainly to focus on verse 14 today. The clearest place that we can see God's glory and majesty on earth today is in and through his people, his redeemed sinners, now made saints by grace. How is this so? Let's look at three reasons.

"He has raised up a horn for his people" may sound strange to us. But in ancient times it was a way to speak of strength. Think of an animal like a rhinoceros that uses its horn to fight. It is a sign of power and virility. This phrase means either that God has made his people strong or that he has been their strength. It may mean both. It may mean that God has been our strength which in turn gives us great confidence and hope. Even as we still walk on a fallen planet and are beset by sin, struggle, and sorrow, God's people should have a strong sense and awareness that God is for us. He is fighting our battles. He is carrying our load. We will prevail in the end, if not in this life, in the next life for sure!

The second phrase is strange at first but here is the essential meaning. Even in this life, God raises up praise for his people. As we grow in godliness and are changed and mature, others will see and honor us for that. It won't happen all the time and the praise won't come from all people. But there will certainly be some of it. See 1 Peter 2:12.

But the third reason is the best and where I really want us to focus. God is near us. What does this mean, especially in light of the fact that in some sense God is everywhere? It speaks to three things: relation, attention, and affection.

Relationally, God is near his people. I've taken two of my sons on school field trips before to Washington, D.C. The teachers ask that all parents keep an eye out for the safety of all kids on the trip, which I tried to do. In reality, I kept my eye mainly on my own son. He stood out to me. I felt more responsibility for him. God made all people, loves all people, and blesses all people. And yet he has a special, saving love for his covenant people. He keeps his eye on them in a unique way to bless them in ways that all people don't get to enjoy.

This thought leads us naturally into our next. The fact that God has bound himself to us in a saving relationship means that in a sense he pays more attention to us. He watches over us for our good. Once at a family reunion, sides were being picked for family Olympics. One father there had a son who was not very athletic and sensitive about the fact. The father watched as more and more kids were picked for teams and this son was nearer and nearer to being last. The father's heart ached. He didn't think of other younger cousins in that moment. His heart was bound up with the sensitives and insecurities of his son. Likewise, God is a great Father who is extremely attentive to the needs of our hearts. He knows our innermost thoughts. He is intimately acquainted with all our ways. Cast all your cares on him, for he cares for you (1 Peter 5:7).

Lastly, God has great affection for his people. He cares deeply for us. His heart is bound up with ours. He keeps all our tears in his memory (Psalm 56:8). He is a sympathetic high priest. See Hebrews 2.17 and 4:14–15.

God is so faithful. He has saved us and promised to love us unwaveringly, even as we continue to sin. He is our strength, hope, and confidence. He is loyal in his covenant love to us.

His loyalty to us should inspire, motivate, and strengthen our loyalty to him. But here is our truest hope. Even when we fail and falter, and we often will, he remains faithful. The life, death, and resurrection of Christ is God's signed and sealed promise to us that he will remain faithful to us in salvation, even as we often fumble in our faithfulness to Him. This, more than anything else, should renew our love and loyalty to him in all times and seasons!

## READ AND REMEMBER

Read Psalm 148 once.

## ASK AND ANSWER

Write down any thoughts or questions here.

## WRITE AND WORSHIP

Make this psalm your own. Write it out in your own words based on your own circumstances and life experience. Celebrate God's faithfulness here. Focus exclusively on praise today, with minimal to no prayer requests. End by singing the hymn out loud if you can.

## IMMORTAL, INVISIBLE

by Walter Chalmers Smith

Immortal, invisible, God only wise, In light inaccessible hid from our eyes, Most blessed, most glorious, the Ancient of Days, Almighty, victorious Thy great name we praise.

Unresting, unhasting, and silent as light, Nor wanting, nor wasting, Thou rulest in might; Thy justice, like mountains, high soaring above Thy clouds, which are foundations of goodness and love.

To all, life Thou givest to both great and small, In all life Thou livest the true life of all; We blossom and flourish as leaves on the tree, And wither and perish but naught changeth Thee.

Great Father of glory, pure Father of light, Thine angels adore Thee, all veiling their sight; All praise we would render O help us to see 'Tis only the splendor of light hideth Thee! Amen.

## LISTEN AND LEARN

Write any final insights here.

# Conclusion

## What to Do Next?

I recently had a conversation with my teenage daughter. She said, "Dad, I read my Bible and journal everyday but I don't feel like I have a real relationship with God. What do you do?"

We had a great conversation after that about the gospel, which she did understand. We talked about assurance of salvation. We also talked about experiencing God through the word and prayer.

I told her to imagine that I went on a long mission trip to a place like the mountains of Haiti where there were no phones, no cell service, and no Wi-Fi. But we were able to mail letters back and forth. We love each other, so we would probably write often. If she received a letter from me, she would read it in a personal way with affection and not just like a history book from school. Likewise when she wrote a letter back to me it would be personal and interactive. If I had asked her a question in my letter such as "How has soccer practice been going?" she would probably answer it in her letter.

I used that illustration to help her see that though the Bible obviously contains true history, it is not mainly given to us as an academic text book. It is right to think of it as a love letter from God. It is more than that. It is not less than that. When she and all Christians read the Bible, they should read it as the God of all creation speaking to them personally (and corporately with other Christians as well.) Again, the Bible is more than that. But it is not less than that.

Then when she, and all Christians pray, at least part of their communication with God ought to be in response to what he said to them in his word. We should not pray in such a way that totally ignores all God has said to us. John Piper essentially says the same thing in a slightly different way as he comments on John 15:7:

> [W]elcome Jesus into our lives and make room for him to live, not as a silent guest with no opinions or commands, but as an authoritative guest whose words and priorities and principles and promises matter more to us than anything else does. . . He doesn't intend for our thinking about his words to replace fellowship with him through his words. He intends for musing on his words to be fellowship with him. We hear the words of Jesus as living words spoken by a living person. It is a spiritually intentional act of relating to a living person when you take his words into your mind. This is what it means for his words to abide in us.[1]

My goal in this study has been to provide an easy to use, easy to remember way to do that. I hope that it has been helpful. I once heard a friend say, "Methods are many, principles are few. Methods always change, principles never do." This is perhaps another way to say "There's more than one way to skin a cat." There are some eternal principles in life all people should live by. I believe it's fair to say all Christians should ideally spend time in the word and prayer every single day if at all possible. But exactly how this should be done can have many varied answers. This short devotional has tried to share one tried and true example. If it hasn't been helpful, feel free to discard it and find a better way. Maybe it'll serve as a creative springboard to launch you into better personal methods of Bible meditation and prayer.

I had a conversation with a good friend yesterday who's in his fifties. He's an officer in his church. He said his main struggle in life is belief. There are times when he doubts if God is even real because God so often does not feel near to him, nor personal to him. He

---

1. Piper, *When I Don't Desire God*, 107.

also confessed his time alone with God has been very up and down and sporadic.

There is a symbiotic relationship between our faith in God, our experience of God, and our discipline of seeking God. Usually the three go up together or go down together. It is not a tit for tat relationship. It doesn't mean if you read the Bible one day you are guaranteed a great experience that day. Nor does it mean if you skip your Bible reading and have doubts the next day that God can't manifest himself to you in a very powerful way that same day. But over the whole span of your life your faith in God, experience of God, and discipline in seeking God will play off of one another and effect one another for better or worse.

Imagine if we lived during World War I. If two married men both had to leave for Europe for years to fight it would be hard to stay in touch with their wives. Imagine one man and wife literally wrote letters to one another daily. They eagerly received, read, and treasured every letter. The other couple, for whatever reasons, rarely, if ever wrote one another.

Two years later it is likely that the first couple would miss one another greatly but would also still maintain a strange degree of intimacy and closeness through their communication. The couple that never communicated with any consistency would feel so distant. They might even feel like they didn't know one another anymore. I'm concerned this is how many modern professing believers feel towards God in heaven. Please don't let that be you.

My idea in writing this book was to give people at least a one month tool to hopefully build some consistent habits in Bible study and prayer and worship. If it has been helpful consider a few options on how to move forward from here to further solidify whatever good you've gleaned from this book.

Option one is to go back through the whole book again and if you didn't use all the space for writing, force yourself to slow down more and write more and fill the pages with your questions, thoughts, journals, prayers, meditations, and insights. Option two, if you did fill all or most of the writing spaces up with your prayers and meditations then buy a blank journal of some sort and go back through the book again and fill up a new journal.

Option three is for those who might find that going through the exact same 31 psalms for another 31 days in a row seems too redundant. If that's you, start back at psalm 1 and go chronologically through the whole book trying to do one psalm a day. You can always split up psalms that are longer such as Psalm 119.

Option four; start with Psalm 5 (the first Psalm this book skipped) and go through the psalms chronologically, skipping all the psalms addressed in this book. If you choose to do either option three or four, I'd highly recommend Tim and Kathy Keller's devotional on the Psalms called the *Songs of Jesus* to use for your context each day.

Option five, choose another book of the Bible, maybe 1 Samuel, John, Philippians, or Ephesians. Then apply the same principles here in the CRAWL acronym to study, pray, meditate, and worship through that book. Whatever you do, take the time every day to go deep in your personal relationship with your Savior!

# Bibliography

Calvin, John. *Commentary on the Book of Psalms, vol. 1.* Translated by James Anderson. Grand Rapids, MI: Baker Book House, 2003.

———. *Institutes of the Christian Religion 1 & 2,* edited by John T. McNeill. Louisville, KY: Westminster John Knox.

Chisholm, Thomas O. "Great is Thy Faithfulness." In *The Hymnal for Worship and Celebration,* 43. Waco, TX: Word Music.

Collins, John C. "Psalms." In *ESV Study Bible,* edited by Lane T. Dennis, 935–1128. Wheaton, IL: Crossway Bibles, 2008.

Craigie, Peter C and Marvin E. Tate, *Word Biblical Commentary 19: Psalms 1–50.* Nashville, TN: Thomas Nelson, 2004.

Davis, John Jefferson. *Meditation and Communion with God: Contemplating Scripture in an Age of Distraction.* Downers Grove: IVP Academic, 2012.

Friedman, Thomas. *Thank You for Being Late: An Optimist's Guide to Thriving in the Age of Accelerations.* New York, NY: Farrar, Straus and Giroux, 2016

Gil, John. *Psalms.* Albany, OR: AGES, 1999.

Henry, Matthew. *The NIV Matthew Henry Commentary.* Grand Rapids, MI: Zondervan, 1992.

Lewis, C. S. *Letters to Malcolm Chiefly on Prayer.* New York, NY: Harcourt Brace Jovanovich, 1963

Lloyd-Jones, D. Martyn. *Spiritual Depressions.* Grand Rapids, MI: Eerdmans, 2002.

Keller, Timothy. *Prayer.* New York, NY: Dutton, 2014.

———. *Praying with the Psalms.* New York, NY: Redeemer Presbyterian Church, 2008.

———. *The Songs of Jesus* New York, NY: Viking, 2015.

Kidner, Derek. *Psalms 1–72.* Downers Grove, IL: IVP, 2008.

———. *Psalms 73–150.* Downers Grove, IL: IVP, 2008.

MacArthur, John. *The MacArthur Study Bible.* Nashville, TN: Word, 1997.

Mathis, David. *Habits of Grace.* Wheaton, IL: Crossway, 2016.

Mote, Edward. "The Solid Rock." In *The Hymnal for Worship and Celebration,* 402. Waco, TX: Word Music.

Motyer, Alec. *Psalms by the Day.* Ross-shire, Scotland: Christian Focus, 2016.

———. "Psalms" In *New Bible Commentary,* edited by G. J. Wenham and J. A. Mortyer, 485–583. Downers Grove, IL: IVP, 2004

# Bibliography

Muller, George. *Autobiography of George Mueller*, edited by Fred Bregen. London: J. Nisbet, 1906.

Oatman Jr., Johnson, "Count Your Blessings." In *The Hymnal for Worship and Celebration*. 563. Waco, TX: Word Music.

Ortlund, Dane C. *Deeper*. Wheaton, IL: Crossway, 2021

Newton, John. *The Works of John Newton*. London: Hamilton, Adams and CO, 1824.

Packer, J.I. *Knowing God*. London: Hodder and Stoughton, 1973.

Parrish, Archie. *A Simple Way to Pray*. Atlanta, GA: Serve International, 2002.

Piper, John. *When I Don't Desire God*. Wheaton, IL: Crossway, 2004.

Poole, Matthew. *Commentary on the Holy Bible, vol. 2*. Peabody, MA: Hendrickson.

Snyder, James L. *In Pursuit of God*. Camp Hill, PA: Christian, 1991.

Spurgeon, C. H. *The Treasury of David, vol. 1, part 1*. Peabody, MA: Hendrickson.

———. *The Treasury of David, vol. 1, part 2*. Peabody, MA: Hendrickson.

———. *The Treasury of David, vol. 2, part 1*. Peabody, MA: Hendrickson.

———. *The Treasury of David, vol. 2, part 2*. Peabody, MA: Hendrickson.

———. *The Treasury of David, vol. 3, part 2*. Peabody, MA: Hendrickson.

Stead, Louisa M. R. "'Tis So Sweet to Trust in Jesus." In *The Hymnal for Worship and Celebration*. Waco, TX: Word Music.

Tripp, Paul David. *Lead*. Wheaton, IL: Crossway, 2020.

Made in the USA
Coppell, TX
08 December 2023